T0375152

The Possibility Coaches' Guide™ to

Living an Inspired, Empowered, and Joy-filled Life!
365 Daily Tips to Get You There!

Jon Satin and Chris Pattay

BALBOA.
PRESS
A DIVISION OF HAY HOUSE

Balboa Press books may be ordered through booksellers or by contacting:

Balboa Press
A Division of Hay House
1663 Liberty Drive
Bloomington, IN 47403
www.balboapress.com
1-(877) 407-4847

Because of the dynamic nature of the Internet, any web addresses or links contained in this book may have changed since publication and may no longer be valid. The views expressed in this work are solely those of the author and do not necessarily reflect the views of the publisher, and the publisher hereby disclaims any responsibility for them.

The author of this book does not dispense medical advice or prescribe the use of any technique as a form of treatment for physical, emotional, or medical problems without the advice of a physician, either directly or indirectly. The intent of the author is only to offer information of a general nature to help you in your quest for emotional and spiritual well-being. In the event you use any of the information in this book for yourself, which is your constitutional right, the author and the publisher assume no responsibility for your actions.

Any people depicted in stock imagery provided by Thinkstock are models, and such images are being used for illustrative purposes only.
Certain stock imagery © Thinkstock.

ISBN: 978-1-4525-4253-9 (sc)
ISBN: 978-1-4525-4252-2 (hc)
ISBN: 978-1-4525-4254-6 (e)

Library of Congress Control Number: 2011960530

Printed in the United States of America

Balboa Press rev. date: 11/17/2011

"The true indicator of a life well-lived is not about what you are doing or where you are going; it is about how far you've come from yesterday to today!"

~

Jon Satin and Chris Pattay

The Possibility Coaches

Acknowledgments

Thank you to all our teachers and mentors. We want to extend a special "thank you" to those individuals who were extremely influential in our personal transformations over the last two decades: Dr. John Falbo, Jeffrey Combs, Dr. Wayne W. Dyer, Marianne Williamson, Louise L. Hay and Eckhart Tolle.

We very much appreciate the support we have received from family, friends and colleagues.

Finally, thank you to all the courageous men and women who have decided to awaken to their magnificence and for choosing The Possibility Coaches as their guides.

How to Use This Book

Real positive change is possible. Yes, it's true! You have the power to move your life in any direction you want it to go. However, doing so requires your participation and commitment to the process of personal growth and transformation.

Based on our experiences and personal transformations during this incredible journey called Life, we have created a treasury of what we call "Daily Tips." These "tips" are guideposts to use each day as reminders to you about who you are becoming as a person and as a contributor to the world we live in.

To receive the most benefit from this book read one tip per day. Although the tips are numbered 1 through 365, you can start this book at any time throughout the year at tip number 1. We suggest reading your daily tip first thing in the morning. Then, throughout your day, reflect upon the message and content of the tip and consider applying its' wisdom to your daily activities. Then watch the magic happen!

We believe with our hearts and souls that when you read and apply our tips and practice their messages with the intent and desire to be the living embodiment of what they each teach and represent, you will witness miraculous changes in both your life and your life situations.

Our daily tips may make you smile, laugh or cry. They may stir you a bit or a lot. They may actually move you to begin to question the path you are taking. They may even awaken you! However, it is our intent, as your guides, that our tips have a profound, positive effect on you.

To Your Success, Joy and Happiness!

Jon Chris

The Possibility Coaches

1

Tip of the Day

"Release the idea today of having a 'perfect' reputation!"

Worrying about how the world sees you adds stress and anxiety to your life. Focusing on perfection blocks you from being who you are at your core. Adopt this mantra today: *'What you think of me is none of my business!'* Say it over and over, day in and day out! Believe this statement and you free yourself from the need to prove your worthiness. Know that the only opinion regarding *you* that counts is your own.

Eliminate the need to have a perfect reputation today.

2

Tip of the Day

"Be open to being less controlling today!"

Select one person, situation or outcome in your life that you are attempting to manipulate and let them or it go. Commit to this for 24 hours. Just one day! Tomorrow see if you awaken less drained, more energized, relaxed and even at peace.

Let go of being controlling today and begin the process of trusting that all is well in your world.

3

Tip of the Day

"To have a winning life today you must first stop whining!"

Being a victim prevents you from moving forward and living a happy, fulfilled life. When you blame and complain you give your power away to people, events and circumstances. That is called self-disempowerment. Reverse the process and become empowered.

Take responsibility today and begin the process of winning in the game of life.

4

Tip of the Day

"Believe in others today even if they do not believe in themselves!"

At one time in your life you may have had someone who believed in you even when you may have been 'down and out.' Can you recall how uplifting it was to have a cheering squad move you forward? Inspire someone today to take one action step in their life that creates positive change. Stand by them. Hold their hand if you have to. Be a coach or guide for them so they can begin to awaken to their greatness.

Empower someone by believing in them today.

5

Tip of the Day

"Stop trying to 'fix' and 'save' people today!"

Despite what you may think, these are exhausting processes that will always be less than satisfying. In fact, they are more likely to create frustration and stress in your life. We are all on a life journey that has some significant purpose. Within each purpose is the Lesson to be received. 'Fixing' and 'saving' is about the need to control. This interferes with the Life learning process of another person. It's like taking an exam for someone else: in the end no one gains the wisdom required to be truly happy.

Eliminate the need to fix and save from your life today.

6

Tip of the Day

"Choose wisely what you give to the world today!"

The world is like a gigantic mirror. It reflects back to you exactly what you give. *Giving is not only material things.* Your thoughts, words, emotions and actions are all forms of 'giving.' They will determine the results you receive in your life. What you give out dynamically you will attract magnetically.

Focus on giving what you want to receive today.

7

Tip of the Day

"Take money out of the equation that is your life situation today!"

When money is the main reason for living, your power is given away. Money and the abundance or lack of it, is an end result of an exchange of energy through service. Put service first and you live authentically at the level of cause. Living at the 'level of cause' means you are empowered to create the reality that you want for your life! Ironically, then, more money will appear in your life.

In the equation of your life situation today, put service first and watch money appear.

8

Tip of the Day

"The people in your life today are part of your life's classroom curriculum!"

Life never gives you what you cannot handle and that includes people. People show up in your life for a reason, never by chance. They all have a purpose that can, with your permission, assist you to grow. The relationships you share with them are part of the journey to achieving inner peace.

Bless everyone in your life today.

9

Tip of the Day

"Who is living in your head today?"

Is it happiness, gratitude, appreciation and joy? Or is it anger, resentment, frustration and apathy? Your mind is a piece of real estate that you own and are responsible for maintaining. You are also responsible for who you allow in as tenants. If you do not like who is living in your head give them an eviction notice.

Take inventory of who is living in your head today.

10

Tip of the Day

"Give up being afraid of being happy today!"

As insane as this may sound it is valid and true for most people. Happiness appears to be this elusive state of being that we search to find. The truth is happiness is avoided because to genuinely be happy would contradict a life that is perceived as a struggle, full of strife and challenges.

Examine your relationship with happiness today and ask why you may actually fear it.

11

Tip of the Day

"Beginning today, view so-called 'setbacks' as growth spurts in disguise!"

In life we encounter people, situations and events that on the surface appear to be setbacks. Life happens! It is what it is; however, your response to the everyday experience determines how you view people and circumstances. Setbacks are guideposts and opportunities to view life differently.

Change your perspective today by viewing setbacks as growth spurts.

12

Tip of the Day

"Realize today that anger is a symptom of the need to judge!"

All anger is a symptom of the addiction to be judgmental. Judging is used to make ourselves feel and look better. It is rooted in the false belief that 'if I make others appear small and inadequate I will feel and appear big and special.' The flaw in this thinking is you must always seek a source of anger. How emotionally exhausting is that?

Stop judging today and watch your anger subside.

13

Tip of the Day

"Enjoy your life today!"

No amount of success will create happiness, joy and peace in your life if you dislike the process. Decide what *'fun'* is for you! Identify your values and passions. Welcome them as conditions for living your life from the *'inside-out.'* When you set an intention that contains a component of joy, you will experience fulfillment.

Commit to having fun by being joyful today.

14

Tip of the Day

"Notice how you are feeling today!"

Feelings are the fuel that feed your creative abilities. How you feel is critical to the process of achieving your goals. You want to feel good...it is that simple! Consciously create positive feelings like happiness, gratitude, appreciation and excitement. Pay close attention to the overall nature of how you are feeling now. This determines the level of fullness and quality of the life you are living.

Notice the status of how you are feeling today.

15

Tip of the Day

"Stop worrying about whether or not people like you!"

You are not a child anymore. Stop participating in popularity contests. Switch gears and begin to focus on receiving respect from others. The quickest way to receive respect is to first give it to you. When you respect yourself people energetically feel the value you place upon yourself. The result is that they will respond in kind by respecting you.

Respect who you are today.

16

Tip of the Day

"Choose happiness today!"

Happiness is not, as most believe, some destination, relationship or situation to strive to get so we can feel complete, whole and wanted. Happiness is simply this: *a choice we make about how we feel in any given moment.* It's an '*inside job,*' so choose wisely.

You are one thought, one decision away from being happy today.

17

Tip of the Day

"Eliminate stress from your life today!"

How many times a day do you say: "I'm so stressed!"? Do you really know what that means when you exclaim that statement? By stating out loud or even silently thinking that you are stressed creates a continuous focus on and an attachment to future events and situations. The solution: be present and mindful about what you are doing right here and now.

By giving one hundred percent to this moment you have begun the process of stress elimination in your life today.

18

Tip of the Day

"Open the door today because opportunity is knocking!"

Do you believe great opportunities come around once in a while or even once in a lifetime? The truth is opportunity is a function of who you are as a creative being. To make the most of opportunities means you awaken and see each encounter and experience as a chance to create and collaborate with others.

Open the door today and welcome opportunity into your life.

19

Tip of the Day

"Realize today that there is no such thing as failure... only feedback!"

Life always gives you feedback. This is how we learn to create results that we desire. We receive the same undesirable results time and time again when we choose to ignore the feedback Life gives to us.

Create new results in your life by observing and acknowledging the feedback you receive today.

20

Tip of the Day

"The people in your life today will do what you do, not what you say!"

Those you have influence over: your children, staff at work, employees, will do what you do or not do what you are not willing to do. When you want others to take action or create changes be willing to *'walk the talk'* otherwise, you will find yourself challenged and frustrated.

'Walk your talk' today and see your world change.

21

Tip of the Day

"Show people how much you care about them today!"

Be willing to go the extra mile. Put your heart into assisting others. Focus on their success. Lend a hand. Lift someone up. Do a good deed. Now watch your life becomes more enriched. Another person's success is also your success. People do not care about how much you know... they want to know how much you care!

Go that extra mile for someone today.

22

Tip of the Day

"Be glad today for another person's success!"

Jealousy and envy are barriers to true happiness and success. Feeling these emotions promotes a belief system in you that says 'their gain is my loss.' This implies that there is not enough to go around. Begin to consider and eventually accept that there is an unlimited supply of whatever it is you desire: be it money, love or success.

Now that you know there is enough for everyone, be happy for someone else today.

23

Tip of the Day

"You got out of bed this morning; however, are you awake today?"

To be truly awake requires awareness. Be aware of your thoughts and their content. Do they make you feel good or not so good? Be aware of how you act and react to events and situations. Ask yourself: *'Why do I have these thoughts and why do I act and react the way I do?'* Listen for the answers! You are now awakening. Good Morning!

Your conscious awareness guarantees that you are awake today.

24

Tip of the Day

"Be enlightened today!"

Enlightenment is not some far-off state of consciousness. It requires 3 simple, yet not necessarily easy steps. They are: *1. Cease all judgment of others and yourself, 2. Cease attaching your happiness to other people and outcomes and 3. Cease resisting Life and accept 'what is' in any given moment.*

Follow this process and you will find your peace today and perhaps witness a few miracles, too.

25

Tip of the Day

"Memorialize those who came before us by thanking them today!"

With gratitude, let us remember those who preceded us and who contributed to uplifting humankind in their own special way. However they demonstrated it, each of them had the strength, courage and belief that it is everyone's right to be free on all levels of life: physically, emotionally and spiritually. By recognizing what we have now, because of those who gave on our behalf, we are uplifted and inspired to use our talents for the betterment of our world.

Give thanks today to those we respect and admire from yesterday.

26

Tip of the Day

"Acknowledge your greatness today!"

Give up thinking and playing 'small.' Within you are seeds of potential to create wonderful results. Deny your greatness and you deny your true power. Your greatness is your capacity to love and be loved. It is not disease or death you fear most. It is your greatness. Greatness contradicts struggle which you believe is a necessary feature of life. Know that struggle is neither essential, nor noble! End the struggle and watch your seeds of greatness germinate and grow.

Say 'Yes' to your greatness today.

27

Tip of the Day

"Be authentic today!"

Authenticity is more than being real, honest and upfront with others. It is about being true to you. It is also about creating an outer, physical world that reflects who you are at your core...the heart and soul that's 'YOU'. Do not deprive yourself of the experience of being authentic. It will block you and the world from evolving both physically and spiritually.

Free yourself and the world by practicing authenticity today.

28

Tip of the Day

"Begin an intimate relationship with yourself today!"

If you want an intimate relationship with another person we suggest you first focus on having one with yourself. The truth is if you have a challenge being intimate with you, how can you expect to be intimate with someone else? Go on a date with yourself. Spend a few hours a week out by yourself. *Know yourself now!* Enjoy your company!

Raise the level of intimacy you have with you today.

29

Tip of the Day

"Practice patience today!"

As the saying goes *'Patience is a virtue'* and let us add that patience suggests being 'grounded.' Being *'grounded'* means you know that results and situations you want occur at the 'perfect' time in your life. Impatience implies lack of trust and attachment to outcomes. It is also resistance to change and learning what you need to know. Impatience is a huge barrier to manifesting what you want for your life.

Be more virtuous by creating a new habit of patience today.

30

Tip of the Day

"Acknowledge and thank your teachers today!"

The teachers we are referring to here are not the educated and certified school pros who give you facts and figures to memorize. We are referring to the teachers we call your *'button pushers.'* Those who 'get to you' by what they say, do or how they even look at you. As difficult as it may be, begin to thank them with profuse gratitude. Thank them for revealing to you the specific traits you have that may require closer examination. This process is required for your personal as well as your professional evolution. Bless those who seem to make you crazy!

Thank your real teachers today.

31

Tip of the Day

"Examine your 'core' beliefs today!"

Your core beliefs are those beliefs you possess that determine how you see yourself and your relationship to the world. Ask yourself: '*What are my beliefs about my key relationships: with others, myself and with money?*' Write them down. The results may cause you to consider creating changes. Now, ask yourself: '*Where did my beliefs come from?*'

Begin to question the validity and truthfulness of your core beliefs by examining them today.

32

Tip of the Day

"Choose to live your life from absolute truths today!"

Rather than living life that is based on beliefs, rumors and half-truths, live your life from what you know to be true beyond the shadow of a doubt. Most of our beliefs are assumptions and if we allow them to, they dictate our reality. Beliefs are not caused, they are created by choice. 'Belief about something is not the same as its existence.' Do you believe you can drive a car or do you know it as absolute truth? A knowing is experiential. A belief is a perception that can distort the way you think and act every minute of every day. End distortions by living life based on what you know.

Let your absolute truths guide you, today.

33

Tip of the Day

"Tap into, infuse and ignite some passion into your day today!"

Most people believe that passion comes from external events like 'If I had the right career then I would be passionate about it.' Not true! Passion is within you, either dormant or active. It comes in a variety of forms ranging from love and desire to anger and rage. Passion creates excitement. Passion breeds enthusiasm. To experience passion, it is essential that you connect with your feelings. Move out of your head and into your heart.

Give yourself permission to explore your passions today.

34

Tip of the Day

"Recognize that you have the power of 'free will'...so make the most of it today!"

You have the freedom to claim your goodness. Your goodness is divinely and rightfully yours, as it is for all other people. What you receive for your life and in your lifetime is determined by the choices and decisions you make daily. No other species in the natural world has this ability to create its reality. You are the pilot of your life's course. Make the choices and decisions that result in an enjoyable flight. It may not always be free of turbulence; however, know that wherever you ultimately 'land' is up to you.

Exercise the power of your free will on your journey of your life today.

35

Tip of the Day

"Take your focus off of 'getting it all done' today by tapping into the creative energy field that is you!"

Do you realize that you will never get 'it' all done? Do you even know what 'it' is? Life is a journey and a process. It is about creating. Memorize this equation: *Creation=Evolution.* Decide here and now what it is you want to create. Decide in this moment how you would like to evolve in this lifetime. Allow the creative process to flow through you.

Shift your focus to the creative power you are today and watch your life evolve into the masterpiece it is intended to be.

36

Tip of the Day

"Move from living in your head to living in your heart today!"

Living in your head is all about thinking, analyzing and 'trying to figure it all out.' Living in your head is quite likely going to lead you to non-action, indecision, chaos and procrastination. *Understand that where you are today is the result of your 'best' thinking.* When we live in our heart we can only hear and live from the Truth. Your heart never leads you astray into dead-end results. Your heart is your core, your soul, the music that is your life yet to be played.

To create real, positive change in your life, move into and live from your heart today.

37

Tip of the Day

"Know your intentions today!"

Consciously or not, you are always setting intentions. An intention is a compass. In modern, technological terms, an intention can be likened to a car's GPS. You set intentions to achieve and arrive at a particular goal, outcome, result or destination. To create a desired ending requires you to clearly set your intention. This is your personal GPS. A clear intention requires fortitude, emotional discipline and commitment.

Focus on how you want your life to unfold today and you will achieve goals that put a smile on your face tomorrow!

38

Tip of the Day

"Awakening from sleep today and every day represents a fresh start for your life!"

Each day provides you with a new beginning. It gives you a new lease on life. It also gives you a new supply of unlimited energy. This energy flow can be used to reinvent yourself, redefine your priorities, refocus on your goals, reestablish relationships and boundaries and revitalize your imagination to create whatever it is you desire to be, do or have in this lifetime.

Make the most of a new beginning, today.

39

Tip of the Day

"Remove 'trying' from your life today!"

How many times a day do you say the words 'I'll try...'? Trying always feels less than enthusiastic. Trying can best be defined as *'failing with honor.'* When someone says 'I'll try,' no matter what the subject, they are really saying that 'at this time this is not a priority or important to me.' It reflects a lack of commitment. Stop 'trying!'

Starting today, only make commitments to the people and circumstances you are willing to give one hundred percent to, and then begin to notice how you 'succeed with honor.'

40

Tip of the Day

"Adopt a new, healthy habit today!"

Choosing a new, healthy habit creates instant change in your life. One new habit shifts your perspective and you begin to see yourself differently. Ask yourself: *"Do my current habits reflect who I am or desire to become?" "How do these habits serve me?"* Be brutally honest with yourself! Choose one habit that does not reflect your greatness and exchange it for one that does.

Improve the quality of your life today by selecting and implementing a new, healthy habit.

41

Tip of the Day

"Be encouraging today!"

Any gesture on your behalf to give encouragement to someone implies you are sharing hope and supplying confidence where it may be lacking. The etymology of the word encouragement literally means 'coming from the heart' to support and assist others, as well as yourself. A little bit of encouragement can go a long way and have a huge impact on someone's life.

Live, give and come from the heart today, by practicing encouragement.

42

Tip of the Day

"Know that the only limitation you possess today from living the life you desire is 'FEAR'!"

Fear is the number one reason why people stay 'stuck' in jobs, relationships and dead-end situations. Ask yourself: *"What is it that I am afraid of?"* The answer may surprise you. Is it change? Is it failure? Is it success? Is it happiness? First, know your fear! Then, choose to remove the barriers that created it. By courageously facing your fear you will be inclined to take more inspired, productive action.

Remove any darkness present in your life by shining the light on your fear today.

43

Tip of the Day

"All healthy relationships begin with you today!"

True success requires healthy relationships. Without healthy relationships you cannot be successful. Aim to make friends with everyone you meet. This does not mean you have to call, email or text message them all the time. It does mean that you are willing to put relationships first. This is what *'being of service'* in life and career is all about.

Begin creating healthy relationships today.

44

Tip of the Day

"Create results today that are backed by love!"

Love is our universal intention. Your purpose is unconditional love. Goals that are not backed by love are inauthentic. Without love, the possession of 'things,' money, fame, power and influence have no value. Love, like success, is not a destination. Yet, it is the only true starting point. It is the only energy source that you carry within you that inspires, excites and strengthens you.

Commit to having all the moments that make up your day today, backed by the power of love.

45

Tip of the Day

"Clear time in your schedule today for moments of inspiration!"

Set aside some personal time to be inspired by writing an '*inspiration log.*' List the people you love to be with. Write down the people who inspire you and the activities you love to participate in. Carry this log with you and refer to it often. By focusing on this log you will begin to shift and move toward a greater connection with who you are at your core. It is like a catalog of self-rediscovery for you. To create authentic success in your life review your inspiration log daily.

Become aware of the people and activities that inspire you today.

46

Tip of the Day:

"Consider writing a new script today for the movie called 'My Life'!"

Your current thoughts and beliefs are the script you have written for your life up until this very moment. With these thoughts and beliefs, you have created a common, routine, predictable and very familiar script. Now, in addition to being the writer of this movie, you are also the producer, director and its star. You therefore have the power to edit, rewrite, recast or simply toss this script into the trash and start a fresh, new one from scratch. By creating a new script and even cast changes, you may want to consider changing the title of your movie to *'My Incredible Life!'*

Create a box office hit for the movie that is your life today.

47

Tip of the Day

"Tap in to your wisdom today!"

Wisdom is about creating a deeper, richer relationship with you. Take an inventory of your positive traits and characteristics, skills and talents. You may also want to review some of those 'darker' places that may require some immediate attention. Wisdom is about being aware of who you are now and who you are becoming. It is also about knowing where you are and where you are going, and yet simultaneously trusting the process of life by *'living in the mystery.'*

Use your wisdom 'wisely' today.

48

Tip of the Day

"Clean out the cluttered closets in your mind today!"

Like a cluttered home, a cluttered mind can create a feeling of overwhelm, chaos and disorder. To clean your mind, be open to discarding and eliminating items that occupy too much space and have no positive purpose or value. Some of these items you may choose to toss into the trash are guilt, control, judgment, grudges, worry, the 'right to be right,' past mistakes, heartbreaks and emotional wounds. Be willing to let go of these 'internal possessions' in the closets of your mind.

Become a 'feng shui' master for your soul today.

49

Tip of the Day

"Be courageous and watch how it benefits you and others today!"

A life of success requires taking risks. Risk requires courage. *Courage* is from the French '*la coeur*' which means '*the heart*;' therefore, courage and heart are the same driving force. Ask yourself these questions today: "How can I be more courageous in my daily productivity?" "How can I be more courageous in my relationships?" "How can I be more courageous when it comes to how I see myself and my world?" Take a risk! Step out of the box!

Have a heart and be courageous today.

50

Tip of the Day

"Be peace-filled today!"

If you are feeling a bit challenged and/or unclear about your life and your future, this is the one intention we suggest you focus upon today. Beyond all other goals, aspirations, inspirations, motivations and declarations, be at peace! Peace is an 'inside' job and is just one decision away for each of us. No matter how chaotic your life may seem, the most powerful gift you possess is to be peace-filled. By making inner peace your focus you will gain clarity of purpose, vision, focus and a whole new perspective on life!

Give yourself the gift of peace today.

51

Tip of the Day

"Be a great listener when talking to your self today!"

The most important conversations you will have during your lifetime are with yourself. Your self-talk determines how you see the world, the choices you make, actions you take or do not take and how you ultimately live your life. Become an attentive observer of these conversations. Choose to change those conversations that do not encourage or uplift you.

Listen to yourself today and make recommendations for positive change to that person who is YOU.

52

Tip of the Day

"Focus on 'responding' rather than 'reacting' today!"

When you react to what another person says or does or to a certain outcome or situation, you immediately give your power away to that person or situation. Reacting means you are living in a defensive mode, always on guard. This is emotionally exhausting! Conversely, responding is empowering: you consciously, in the moment, move toward a resolution regarding a challenge, disagreement or misunderstanding. As in any sport, becoming a pro at 'responding' takes practice.

'Try-outs' for being a professional responder begin today.

53

Tip of the Day

"Choose a life of success today!"

Success is a journey, not a destination. Consider the type of journey you want to have and be clear about the kind of journey you embark on. Are you on the road *to* success or the road *of* success? Choosing the road *to* success will result in disappointment. You will never 'get there' or 'make it' as your mind promises you. Instead, choose the road *of* success. This is the path where you create and 'act as if' you are the success you seek now. It is where you apply your inner wisdom. This ensures that the luggage you carry on this journey is full of your values and your passions.

Looking forward to seeing you on the 'road of success' today.

54

Tip of the Day

"Today ask 2 key questions to monitor your personal growth!"

In the morning, upon arising, ask yourself: *"What good shall I do today?"* In the evening, upon retiring to bed, ask yourself: *"What good have I done today?"* These two questions will assuredly provide you with clarity of purpose and proof of worthiness. Too often, we focus on what is wrong with our lives and how little or insignificant our presence is to the rest of the world. If that describes a habit you possess, then perhaps it is time to shift gears and begin to focus on the goodness you can share.

Starting today, get in to the habit of asking these two questions and then witness how you are a force for good.

55

Tip of the Day

"Know the truth and importance of your relationships today!"

Your relationships reflect the heart and soul of who you are. They are the building blocks of life; however, they are often forfeited or destroyed in the name of what some may call 'success.' The truth is healthy relationships are the core of 'authentic success.' To completely understand the importance of strengthening your relationships consider these two ideas: Number one: you are unique and number two: know that you are connected to everyone and everything.

This simple shift in perception today can create awesome changes in your life tomorrow.

56

Tip of the Day

"Declare your own personal independence today!"

Declare your independence from worry, fear, struggle and thoughts that no longer serve you. Your personal independence is just a thought away. Be open to releasing the beliefs and habits that keep you locked in and dependent on negative emotions and situations. Decide for emotional and personal freedom. *What a liberating experience!* You may actually begin to enjoy life's bounty.

Take the first step to freedom by declaring your personal independence today.

57

Tip of the Day

"Recommit to your Life today!"

Without exception, this process requires you to look at your fears. You may hold yourself back in life because you choose not to face your fears. Instead, you keep busy, work 'harder' (not smarter), play small and raise the 'noise level' in your life to the 'high' volume setting. Be open to facing one fear today. Shine light on it and see that it has no real positive value.

Create a commitment today to the re-commitment process to living the life you deserve.

58

Tip of the Day

"Re-energize yourself today by raising your levels of inner strength, vitality and resiliency!"

When you lack desire or drive it is more than likely due to emotional, rather than physical exhaustion. One way to reverse these symptoms is to choose to do something for YOU. Self-focus is a sure-fire way to feel renewed. If you do not attend to your needs, who will? To be your best, possess a level of inner strength, vitality and resilience that reflects and supports your emotional well-being.

Re-energize yourself by being self-focused today.

59

Tip of the Day

"Take advice from your heart today!"

The heart is an essential organ for physical life. It's also where Truth and only Truth exists. Conversely, your mind can and will create fear-based stories and illusions for you. Your heart is where your absolute power resides and is linked to everyone and everything. It is the path and the bridge to creation and evolution for our species. It makes absolute sense to listen to the one source of absolute truth that is so powerful and always available to counsel you.

Listen to your heart today.

60

Tip of the Day

"Become aware of the words you use today!"

Your words are a result of what you think and feel. What you think and feel is based upon your beliefs and experiences. The words you speak create your reality. To create what you want, it is important to speak with clarity. State exactly what you want and express it in the present tense. Life gives you exactly what you ask for! Use language that reflects clarity, certainty and faith.

Observe the language you use to express yourself today.

61

Tip of the Day

"Make an 'offering' to another person today!"

An offering is a gift. The type of offer you make to someone is irrelevant as long as the intent is genuine and good. Offer a kind word, an ear, hope, encouragement, comfort, solutions, assistance... the list is infinite. One offering can change another life. One offering has the potential to give you in return, a sense of gratification that you assisted someone on the 'road of success.'

Make an offer that no one could refuse today.

62

Tip of the Day

"Be open to Life today!"

To be open to life requires receptivity. Receptivity requires belief, trust and faith. Openness also indicates an ability to respond to Life instead of reacting to life situations. To respond means presence and the possession of inner peace. To react means closing yourself off to the flow of Life by living in the fight or flight mode.

Tap into your true nature today and see how open to Life you can be.

63

Tip of the Day

"Realize today that you can be successful while you experience fearful thoughts!"

Thoughts are creative if you give them power and nourishment through your feelings and emotions. Thoughts may appear to be random, yet you have the power to change them. Thoughts are by choice. Successful people experience fearful thoughts daily. The difference, however, between successful people and other people is they choose and emotionalize more empowering thoughts. When you experience a fearful thought, act like the successful person you want to be by consciously moving to a loving thought.

Only give your power to positive, loving thoughts today.

64

Tip of the Day

"Step out of your 'comfort zone' today!"

Your comfort zone is where life feels safe, familiar and at ease. Ironically, it is also where you find yourself playing small by creating excuses about *why you are where you are* on life's journey. To play a bigger game, choose something that creates discomfort for you. Next, be willing to go through the process of 'raising the bar' on your comfort level. You may be surprised by the outcome!

Be willing to play in the 'discomfort zone' today in order to create a new level of success for your life.

65

Tip of the Day

"Define success on your own terms today!"

Is your vision of success self-created or was it given to you? What inspires and motivates you is your own personal definition of success for you. You cannot teach yourself success because you already are success! How do you express your success? Your only function is to define success *IN your own terms* and live life *ON your own terms.* Your life 'well-lived' is your expression of what success means to you.

Enjoy successful living today by giving success the definition that is appropriate for you.

66

Tip of the Day

"Observe the content of your conversations today!"

Notice the content of these conversations. Are they valuable, uplifting, empowering, enlightening? Or are they senseless, inauthentic, negative and energy-draining? Topics of conversation that are not enhancing are best left unspoken. In these situations silence is truly golden! Be selective about what you talk about and use discretion. Remember, what you choose to talk about, like what you think about, creates your reality.

Witness your conversations, and when necessary, either change their content or be silent today.

67

Tip of the Day

"Success today begins with taking the first step!"

The first step you take each day on the road of success is your willingness to be open to allowing goodness into your life. When you feel unworthy, wrong or less than perfect, you put up barriers to receiving. These barriers are like detours on the journey of success. Write down one action step right now that reflects your desire to create true success in your life. Then ask yourself how you can complete this action step so you can move in the direction of your desire. Expect an answer. It is waiting for you!

Take your first or perhaps next step of success today.

68

Tip of the Day

"Give up the habit of making assumptions today!"

We tend to make assumptions about everything and everyone. The result of most, if not all assumptions, is that they create misunderstandings. The act of assuming also places us in the position of taking what was said or done, personally. We then end up creating unnecessary drama in our life. From this day forward, eliminate assumptions from your life.

No matter what the circumstances are that you face today, seek to know rather than assume the absolute truth.

69

Tip of the Day

"Focus upon generosity today!"

What truly creates happiness in all of us is the love that emanates from us. When you are generous with your love, everyone will love you. You can never be alone if you are generous. On the other hand, selfishness creates aloneness and loneliness.

Let generosity be your guide as it opens all the doors for you today.

70

Tip of the Day

"Make today and every day an opportunity for personal development!"

This statement does not imply the need for self-improvement. Self-improvement implies that there is something 'wrong' with you. On the other hand, personal development means that you are committed to continuously sharing your gifts with the world. For this commitment to be on-going, you want to be aware of what is going on in your world. Look at what is and is not creating the results you want. Know what is missing and what may be eliminated. Seize the opportunity and take your life to a new level of fulfillment.

Through the process of personal development allow yourself to shine today.

71

Tip of the Day

"Make a list today about what you love about 'the one you love'!"

It is so easy to notice another person's limitations. Truth be said, when you criticize another person, especially someone you care deeply about, from a place of judgment, it can never result in genuine, desired change. All it ever does is keep your mind on someone else and gives you a sense of false power. It is an indicator that your happiness is dependent on another person changing. This creates resentment, hopelessness and frustration. Instead, focus on what you love about your loved one.

Read your 'list' several times today and every day and witness some real miracles appear in your relationships.

72

Tip of the Day

"Give yourself permission today to create positive changes for your life!"

To create real and lasting change it is up to you to allow yourself to embrace change. Change is inevitable so why not move it in a desired direction? This requires that you change your personal permission structure. Your permission structure is like an authority figure in your mind that dictates to you what you can and cannot be, do or have in your life. You are all grown up now! It is time you took charge! If you are seeking changes in your life then you must first change your permission structure.

Make the choice today to give yourself permission to be successful, to thrive and to flourish.

73

Tip of the Day

"Develop appreciation for YOU today... by asking someone who loves you what it is about you they appreciate!"

What others appreciate in you affirms your value and your worthiness. It can be extremely powerful for you to be seen through the eyes of someone who loves you and who is willing to share what they see with you. It is a simple way to remember your uniqueness and goodness.

Ask a loved one today for an 'appreciation assessment.'

74

Tip of the Day

"Decide to be child-like today!"

Being child-like is not being childish or immature. To be child-like is to approach and look at life with a spontaneity and vitality that a child possesses. It is living with an *'anything is possible'* attitude. Recall how a child believes he or she can be anyone or do anything when he or she grows up. Be more child-like.

Imagine, fantasize and dream today about whom you are becoming and what you will do when you grow up.

75

Tip of the Day

"Do not believe yourself today!"

Yes, you read it correctly. Stop believing all the lies you tell yourself. Stop believing those lies that you never chose or wanted to believe, but were programmed and conditioned to believe. Do not believe yourself when you say "I am not good enough, smart enough or strong enough." Do not believe your limitations, unworthiness or that you need to suffer.

Open your heart and listen for the truth about you today.

76

Tip of the Day

"Live without conditions today!"

To go through your day without conditions means you let go of expectations. When you receive today do not worry about how you are going to give back. When you give today do not focus on what you want in return. Living with conditions is living life like it is a contractual agreement. Life is not a contract! Life is love and love has no conditions.

Be unconditional today by living life without conditions.

77

Tip of the Day

"Eliminate setting expectations today for and regarding others!"

Having expectations about other people sets you up for feeling resentment. For your life, you have the right to choose your own level of expectations upon yourself. You decide on your own standards when it comes to what you say or how you behave; however, you do not have that right to impose those standards or behaviors upon others. Give up having expectations where other people are concerned and you will no longer experience anger, resentment and frustration. Instead, it is guaranteed you will feel more at peace.

Eliminate setting expectations today regarding the people in your life.

78

Tip of the Day

"Recognize and then begin to eliminate the '3 Ps' from your life today!"

The 3 Ps are *Perfectionism, Procrastination and Paralysis of Analysis.* The 3 Ps result in avoiding risks and doing anything that could potentially move you toward the results you want. They can also block you from receiving what life has to offer. Be willing to fall down, get up and dust yourself off. This is the process of progress which is the only road of success.

Notice the '3 Ps' today and be willing to release them from your life.

79

Tip of the Day

"Examine yourself today!"

Check to see if the information you carry with you about yourself is inaccurate. Look within today and ask the following questions: "What do I believe about myself?" and "How do I demonstrate this belief?" Your responses will provide you with two key results. The first is a new awareness about you and how you see you. The second result will be the prescription you require for you to create a more positive self-image.

Perform a checkup on YOU today and uncover any inaccurate information about yourself.

80

Tip of the Day

"Let go of your problems today so you can create solutions!"

When you have a so-called 'problem' your mind may race frantically out-of-control. These racing thoughts create so much internal 'noise' that you are unable to hear the guidance available to you from within. Practice quieting your thoughts. This is a skill that requires practice, focus and most of all the mastery of patience.

Distance yourself from your 'problems' today and invite 'solutions' into your life.

81

Tip of the Day

"Be willing to let go of the past today!"

Holding onto the past is like carrying a ball and chain. When you notice yourself judging and criticizing yourself and others, you cannot be present and live life fully. You poison your whole being by feeling guilty, having regrets and holding grudges. Your life becomes a series of *'should haves,' 'wished I hads,' and 'why didn't I's.'* As William Shakespeare wrote, "What's done is done!"

Let go of the past today unless it is a memory that puts a smile on your face.

82

Tip of the Day

"Know what it means to 'have heart' today!"

You have a heart that is essential to your physical existence; however, do you 'have heart?' To have heart means to be inspired and to be enthusiastic. It is the adrenaline that makes you jump out of bed in the morning. It is the love and compassion you have for life and all forms of life, including you. To 'have heart' indicates that you understand that how you treat the world is how the world will treat you.

'Have heart' today and create some real magic.

83

Tip of the Day

"Recognize what it is about you that you love today!"

Self-acknowledgement is an important component for anyone to be truly esteemed. No one or nothing can give you a real, lasting feeling of love for you like you can. Love, like success, is an inside job. Unconditional love is the key to true success.

Identify at least one quality you love about yourself today and apply it to create a positive result for you or someone else.

84

Tip of the Day

"Decide today to design your life out of the choices you make!"

Consciously surround yourself with supportive people and circumstances. Ask yourself if the people in and the conditions of your life support the person you are at your core or the person you have decided to become. If they do not, consider positive action steps and changes. Be creative so that the people in and the conditions of your life reflect the real you.

Design a life today that supports whom you choose to be.

85

Tip of the Day

"Develop the habit today of regularly engaging in conversations to explore possible solutions to so-called problems!"

It is important to maintain an on-going, open dialogue with family, friends, co-workers or employees. The focus of this dialogue must be solution-oriented rather than a gathering of victims or a 'pity party.' This process of brainstorming for solutions allows everyone to participate in an environment that builds individual value and worth.

Lead by example today by creating the habit of welcoming and engaging in solution-oriented conversations.

86

Tip of the Day

"Set aside some time today to focus on what it is you want to be remembered for in this life!"

Too often we put our focus and energies into 'things.' When we do this we give our power away to 'things.' 'Things' are not only material. They are situations, events, and experiences, too. In the end, what really matters most? You will not be eulogized about the car you drove or the size of your financial portfolio. You will be remembered for the love you shared and the capacity in which you served the world.

Focus on love and service today so the memory of you will be etched in the minds of all the lives you touched.

87

Tip of the Day

"Look at all life today, including your own, with reverence!"

To have reverence is to have respect. Too many people lack reverence and thus see the world and Life as cheap and disposable. We see in the animal kingdom how weaker forms of life feed the stronger. We view each other as 'prey' to satisfy our emotional and physical needs. This is a perception that lacks reverence. Reverence is the acceptance that all Life is of valuable. Reverence is an *attitude of gratitude.'* It is also a sign of compassion.

Look at all life forms, including the one you see in the mirror, with reverence today.

88

Tip of the Day

"Look at any crisis or challenge in your life as an opportunity today!"

Whatever it is you may be facing could very well be a blessing in disguise. A challenge in your life, be it a relationship or a situation, is a prompting from your unconditioned self... a sort of kick in the 'you-know-where.' The kick is to let you know that changes in your life are required. Look at your crisis or challenge and ask yourself, "What is the lesson or feedback I am receiving from this situation?" Listen for an answer and ask for guidance. There is a power available to assist you.

Ask, believe and opportunity will be given to you today.

89

Tip of the Day

"Ask your heart what it wants for you today!"

Asking your heart what it desires reconnects you to your authentic self. Take time today and ask yourself: "What is important to me?" "What excites me?" "What do I care about most?" These questions create responses that represent an awakening of who you are at your core.

Spend quality time with your heart today by participating in a 'question and answer' session.

90

Tip of the Day

"Create the future you desire by creating a new level of commitment today!"

The quality of all your tomorrows is influenced by the commitments you make today. You are the designer and architect of your life. Be certain to build a strong foundation!

Commit to being happy and successful today and observe how beautiful your life unfolds tomorrow.

91

Tip of the Day

"Be open to giving and receiving today!"

The process of Life is one of giving and receiving. You cannot have one without the other. We challenge you today to give 3 compliments to others and actually ask for 3 compliments from others about you! *Are you squirming in your seat?* The more uncomfortable this exercise makes you feel, the more resistant you are to the flow of Life.

All the more reason to create positive change by participating in an exercise of giving and receiving today.

92

Tip of the Day

"Reclaim your personal power today by realizing that you are powerful!"

You possess and control the power that determines how you feel, what you see and value and how you act in any situation. To harness this power, however, requires you to be willing to take full responsibility for your life's current status. It also requires you to commit to creating changes that are in alignment with who you truly are! Reclaim your power. Take responsibility. Commit to positive change.

The result will be a joyful YOU bearing witness to the powerful Being you are today.

93

Tip of the Day

"Envision exactly how you want your day to unfold today!"

By seeing how the events of the day occur prior to them becoming reality is a surefire way to create the life you desire today and every day. Focus on the results that give you joy and satisfaction, rather than putting energy into what may go 'wrong.' You are the power behind your physical reality.

Decide on the life you want today and everyday by envisioning the outcomes now.

94

Tip of the Day

"Know what your 'essential needs' are today!"

Recognize your requirements as a human being and distinguish them from artificial needs. You create artificial needs to control, manipulate or to get attention. Having artificial needs means you are needy. When you are needy, happiness is determined by external factors. First, identify these artificial needs from your life. Then, follow up by eliminating them from your life.

By knowing and giving attention to your essential needs today you will realize just how easy they are to obtain.

95

Tip of the Day

"Love your body today!"

There is one body your spirit resides in during this lifetime. You may like it or despise it; yet we suggest you accept it and be grateful for it. Science has proven that our bodies react to our every thought and emotion. Treat your body well and it will respond healthfully. Abuse it, and it will breakdown and decompose. You are the *soul* caretaker of the physical body that houses you.

Physically and emotionally nurture, treat and feed your body well today.

96

Tip of the Day

"Become optimistic about your future today!"

'Flip the switch' by living life from the position of 'I will believe it when I see it' to the powerful stance of '*I will see it when I believe it!*' All physical reality is created by thought. When a thought is backed by belief its likelihood to manifest is quantified beyond reason.

Starting today, believe in the thoughts regarding the life you want and witness some real positive results tomorrow.

97

Tip of the Day

"Check your emotional temperature today!"

Your emotions are your body's reaction to
your thoughts. Physical pain in any area of
your body is a message that your thoughts
are not in alignment with your authentic Self.
By observing and then consciously changing
your thoughts you will begin to see bodily pain
subside and perhaps disappear completely.

Get a reading on your emotional temperature today.

98

Tip of the Day

"Create more awareness in your life today!"

Increased awareness requires you to be the observer of your thoughts and behavior. It is also about observing the people in your life. Awareness is a higher level of consciousness than thinking because it exists in the present moment. Absolute truth only exists in the now, so through the awareness process you can see who you are right here, right now. It can also provide you with clarity regarding who you want to be tomorrow.

Witness Life through awareness today.

99

Tip of the Day

"Put yourself in another person's shoes today!"

Choose someone that is a challenge for you. Be open to seeing the value of that person's position or situation. By being 'in their shoes' you feel their fears and frustrations. This allows the connection between the two of you to rise above the personal to a level of healing that is more fulfilling.

Feel a greater connection by wearing another person's shoes, sandals, sneakers or stilettos today.

100

Tip of the Day

"Become solution-focused today!"

Seeking and creating solutions is a matter of perspective. Being problem focused never creates desired results. In fact, being problem focused actually expands the very situation we want to remove from our lives. On the other hand, being solution-focused means you are willing to give up control. By allowing inspiration to flow through you and events to unfold naturally, the solution process will be revealed to you.

Ask, believe and allow one solution to be delivered to you today.

101

Tip of the Day

"Change your permission structure to achieve a new level of success today!"

To accomplish anything in your life, you first must give yourself permission to achieve it. Part of this structure is the acknowledgment that you are deserving of whatever it is you want to be, do or have. Believing and accepting your worthiness is a prerequisite to receiving.

Give yourself a new permission structure for success today to create new results in your life tomorrow.

102

Tip of the Day

"Pack lightly today for the journey called Life!"

You quite possibly are carrying so much for this journey called Life that it is both physically and emotionally exhausting you. It does not matter if your 'baggage' is 'special' like Louis Vuitton or Coach. If it is weighing you down emotionally or physically, you may want to drop it today! Be willing to lighten the load for the journey called Life.

Pick one piece of emotional baggage and let it go today.

103

Tip of the Day

"Adopt a new philosophy today: What you think about me is none of my business!"

Know that the one and only opinion that counts is yours. How you see YOU, not how others see you, or what they say to you about you, is what matters. Allowing other peoples' opinions to affect how you think, what you believe and how you act, is totally disempowering.

Know that how you think about YOU today is the only opinion that counts.

104

Tip of the Day

"Know that today and every day is a clean slate!"

You can create a new you and a new world today by deciding not to allow all your 'yesterdays' to interfere with the process. Yesterday is history, so consciously choose not to repeat, rehash or relay what happened and who said what to whom. By starting fresh right here and right now you can affect you and your world in so many life-changing ways.

Adopt a 'clean slate' policy for today and every day to come.

105

Tip of the Day

"Give up gossiping today!"

You gossip to make yourself feel better about
yourself. Knowing this one fact about gossiping
will change your perspective. Gossiping is a toxic
addiction. When you judge, criticize, slander another
or pass rumors, the Universe interprets this as an
attack on yourself. Recall the old adage: 'If you
do not have anything nice to say, do not say it!'

*Words to live by as you give
up the urge to gossip today.*

106

Tip of the Day

"Possess a forgiving heart today!"

Choose a situation, challenge or person that is burdensome to you. Know that each person's pain is your pain. Every act of forgiveness completes a life lesson. Ask yourself "What is this situation, challenge or person mirroring back to me?" Knowing the lesson creates compassion. Compassion does not mean you condone inappropriateness. Compassion positions you here and now to let go and forgive.

You have a heart so make it a forgiving one today.

107

Tip of the Day

"Commit to not taking anything personally today!"

The words and actions of others have nothing to do with you. What someone else says or does is a projection or an outpouring of his or her own perception of reality. When you wholly understand this you become totally immune to the opinions, criticisms and behavior of others. As an added bonus, you will begin to eliminate emotional exhaustion from your life.

Be more energized today by not taking anything personal.

108

Tip of the Day

"Before making any decisions today listen to your intuition!"

We all possess great wisdom within us; however, many of us have either abandoned this gift or distrust and totally ignore it. To re-ignite this gift you want to become willing to trust your gut feelings. Practice with small, non-life changing decisions and notice how your intuitive sense is always available to guide you.

Begin to tap in to your intuition today.

109

Tip of the Day

"Give up labels and labeling today!"

When you label a situation, event, relationship, another person or yourself, *your perspective on life is narrow and pigeon-holed.* Labels categorize and compartmentalize. Labeling blocks creativity, limits your ability to grow, keeps you stuck in your head and away from your heart. Stop labeling others and more important, stop labeling you.

Become conscious of the labels you keep in your mind's database today and purge the ones that do not serve or uplift you.

110

Tip of the Day

"Focus on your 'strengths' today!"

Too often we emphasize our so-called weaknesses. We tell ourselves and others about the skills, abilities and capabilities that we lack, have failed at or could not possibly achieve. If this is you, shift gears and focus on your strengths. Hone your skills, resurrect untapped creative abilities and observe the talents that you have ignored for way too long.

Examine and take inventory of your strengths today.

111

Tip of the Day

"See Life through the eyes of someone close to you today!"

In Life, the people closest to us emotionally, tend to become unreal to us. We make assumptions about them by claiming how well we know them and that we know what is best for them. We lose sight that they, like us, have pain and fears. By seeing through a loved one's eyes you will greatly enhance that relationship and become a more compassionate being.

Be open to seeing the world differently today by seeing it with someone else's eyes.

112

Tip of the Day

"Tell someone today how important they are!"

Everyone, without exception, wants to feel important. People are more willing to co-operate and collaborate with you when you make them feel important. As an added bonus, when you assist others and recognize their value you will see your value and importance, too. It is a *'win-win' situation.*

'Make someone's day' today by letting them know that they are important to you.

113

Tip of the Day

"Speak your truth today!"

Your truth is a representation of who you are at the deepest level. It is made up of your desires, hopes, dreams and visions of a life that is lived congruently to your authentic self. When you remain silent and suppress your truth, you stifle the creative expression and flow of who you are.

Say what you feel today and watch your world change before your eyes.

114

Tip of the Day

"Know that every solution you seek to create today is a spiritual 'SOULution' in disguise!"

All so-called problems have *SOULutions.* The fastest way to create a *SOULution* is to simply go through a soul-searching process by tapping into your heart. Your heart always provides a *SOULution* that is best for all concerned.

Turn any problem you have today over to your heart and witness the appearance of the perfect spiritual 'SOULution.'

115

Tip of the Day

"Recognize that your entire history led you to where you are today!"

It is important to let go of the past and to stop living in it. However, it is also as, or even more important to know that all your past experiences have provided you with a tremendous personal advantage. Without the past you could never acknowledge how you have changed, grown and transformed.

Bless your past today and let it go.

116

Tip of the Day

"Deepen your awareness today that we are all in this game called 'Life' together!"

The truth is that all living things are connected. How we navigate through life has a direct effect on countless others. These effects may not appear in an instant, yet they are always unfolding. To see this connection is to see that everyone in your life is part of the chain of goodness. How do we know this? It is so, by virtue of their presence in your life.

Look at the chain of goodness that links you to all life today.

117

Tip of the Day

"Shift from indifference to making a difference today!"

Indifference is apathy and stagnation. It cuts you off from the flow of life. When you switch from the 'I do not care either way' approach to life to *'What can I do?'* and *'Who can I become to make a difference?'* you open doors of multiple opportunities. Stop hiding and wasting the talents you possess.

Make a difference today.

118

Tip of the Day

"Be okay with being happy today!"

Happiness is an inside job. Each of us is just one decision away from happiness. Our world is conditioned to seek out what is 'wrong' and identify it (whatever 'it' is) as the cause of our unhappiness. Being happy seems strange and distant to so many, yet the capacity to experience happiness never leaves us. We have mastered misery and feeling sad; however, would you not prefer to be a happiness expert?

Be happy today just for the heck of it.

119

Tip of the Day

"Thank your favorite 'button pusher' today!"

The *button pushers*. You know who they are. A *'button pusher'* is the one person who causes you to tailspin simply by giving you a look or making a comment. They could say the same thing anyone may say; however, it is only when *they* say 'it' do you unravel. They are one of your teachers and they push your buttons so you can rise above your limitations and truly shine.

Email, text, phone or say 'thank you' in-person to your favorite 'button pusher' today.

120

Tip of the Day

"Give up trying to get 'it' all done today!"

Take time today and look at what it is you are doing. Does it seem like a race with time? Where is the finish line? What happens when you get there? A person who experiences a well-lived life is one who knows that in the whole scheme of life itself, it is the experiences we have that matter most of all. These experiences are based in and reflected by our feelings, emotions and memories. Accept that in this life you are okay with not getting 'it' all done...after all, do you know what 'it' is?

Give up the idea of getting 'it' all done and begin to focus on creating joyous experiences today.

121

Tip of the Day

"Get into the habit of taking action today!"

Most people wait until conditions are 'perfect' to take action; however, those perfect conditions never come to pass. Taking action, even if it feels scary, is the only way to move beyond your fears, gain confidence and achieve results. Do what you fear and watch the fears dissolve. Do not waste time getting ready to act.

Create a new habit today of taking action.

122

Tip of the Day

"Be a skeptic today!"

When you question the validity of what you and others think, believe and say, you may be surprised how your life positively changes for the positive. Skepticism is not doubt or lack of faith. It actually births creative ideas in you. As you begin to question 'truths' and remain open to new answers and solutions you enter new arenas of opportunity. You now broaden your horizons. The impossible becomes possible.

Dare to see where being a skeptic takes you today.

123

Tip of the Day

"Be aware of where you focus your faith today!"

We all have faith in something. There is no such thing as a faithless person. You either have faith in results and situations you desire or in those you do not desire. Ask yourself, *"Do I expect the best or do I expect the worst?"* Either way, you have pointed your faith in one direction or another.

Observe and change if necessary, what you put your faith in today.

124

Tip of the Day

"Know and accept that the process of inner growth precedes what you see in your physical reality!"

There are three phases of inner growth that create the Life you desire: 1. Intentionally focus on good through your thoughts, beliefs and words, 2. Practice patience and detach from your desired outcomes and 3. Witness the desired results appearing in your life.

Create the life you desire by mastering the process of inner growth today.

125

Tip of the Day

"Check your 'trust meter' to know your level of trust today!"

Your level of trust toward people, outcomes and Life is determined by the level at which you trust yourself. Procrastination and indecisiveness are symptoms of a low trust level. Ironically, to raise the level of trust in your life, let go of control and know that you know what is best for you.

Use your 'trust meter' today to measure the level of trust you possess.

126

Tip of the Day

"Do something you fear today!"

You may be resisting this tip already. When you
are willing to face a fear the intention is not
to conquer the fear or complete the task. The
intent is to become aware of how fear operates
within you as a process, keeps you stuck and
depletes you energetically. We actually fear
the fear itself. *Anxiety is the fear of fear.* Be
willing to experience and witness a fear.
We know that you can do it!

Feel and rise above one fear today.

127

Tip of the Day

"Let go of identifying with negativity in your life today!"

When you constantly identify and align yourself with any type of negativity, you are telling yourself on a deeper level that you do not want positive change in your life. Know that negativity pollutes who you truly are. To end negativity, you want to become fully present with yourself. When you notice negativity, view it as a positive message from the Universe that is telling you to shift gears and find a new uplifting point of reference to focus upon.

Move from negativity to positivity today.

128

Tip of the Day

"Act as if today is the last day of your life in this lifetime!"

This may seem bizarre and strange; however, think about it specifically where your relationships are concerned. If this was truly the only day of your life you had, who would you want to talk to, who would you want to see, reconcile with and even forgive? Strong relationships are the key to all levels and types of success in your life. So, what are you waiting for?

Even if it is not the last day of your life, make the most of today by strengthening relationships that have been neglected or even forgotten.

129

Tip of the Day

"Become aware today of the most common symptom of spiritual disconnectedness!"

The most common symptom of spiritual disconnectedness is exhaustion. We also call it 'burnout.' Feeling tired is typically not because of biological or physiological reasons. Exhaustion is Life telling you that your activity plate is overflowing. Ask yourself, "What and who can I remove from my plate that is burning me out and disempowering me?" Clear your plate as needed. Create some down time for you. Then, switch gears and focus on what and who inspires you and designate time for more uplifting experiences.

Turn your exhaustion today into an opportunity for you to reconnect with You.

130

Tip of the Day

"Eliminate problems from your life today by eliminating the word 'problem' from you vocabulary!"

Successful people do not think about, speak of or react to what may appear to those around them as 'problems.' They view any so-called problem as another opportunity to recommit to a desired outcome. Calling a problem an *opportunity* will change your perspective and allow you to expand, grow and take more risks. The result is a more gratifying life lived for you and by you.

Toss out the word 'problem' from your vocabulary and life today.

131

Tip of the Day

"Beware of 'all or nothing thinking' today!"

Do you label your life and your life situations as either all good or all bad? If you do, you likely have a very narrow perspective about you and your life. You are also likely missing a great deal of opportunities for growth and change. Nothing in life is all good or all bad because all things in Life have two sides. To let go of this thought process you want to begin to accept 'what is' in any given moment. It is okay to live in the 'gray' areas of life because that is where you begin to see life differently. Be open to new perspectives and experience synchronistic events that can change the entire course of your life's journey.

Let go of all good or all bad today and open yourself up to opportunities for positive change.

132

Tip of the Day

"Know that your current expectations are the basis for all that you will create today!"

We all have a list of expectations that we live with consciously or not. For most of us, we expect clothes on our backs, food on the table, a roof over our head, a car to drive, etc. Whatever it is that you do not expect in your life will always elude you and stay out of your life. If there is anything or anyone you would like to expect in your life, but have chosen not to consider the possibility of it or them coming into your life, ask yourself 'why?'

Be open to creating new and different expectations today.

133

Tip of the Day

"Choose one habit, situation or person that you are ready and willing to let go of today!"

Affirming your willingness to let go of whatever or whoever it is, is an exercise that speaks volumes to the world. It reflects the mature, compassionate, forgiving and enlightened aspects of who you truly are. It is also a realization for you, by you, that you know that you are worthy of goodness. Anything less, you are willing to release.

Let go of who or what is no longer a positive aspect in your life today.

134

Tip of the Day

"Raise yourself up today!"

Too often in our self-talk and conversations with others we put ourselves down. We tell ourselves we cannot look too good, appear special or accept compliments. Do not fall into the trap that someone else will be there to raise you up. What they think or say about you never takes the place of *your opinion of you!*

Raise yourself up today by telling yourself something about YOU that you love, and accept it as truth.

135

Tip of the Day

"Give up 'the right to be right' today!"

This, above anything you may choose in your life, is the key to inner peace. When you decide to let the rest of the world be a population of 'know-it-alls,' you have found the key that opens the door to your kingdom/queendom of peace. Letting go of the need to be right is extremely liberating.

Commit to giving up 'the right to be right' today and witness positive changes in your life.

136

Tip of the Day

"Witness your anger today!"

Notice how often and how easily you are offended by people, situations and events. Understand that your anger is really caused by something within you that you do not approve of or are unwilling to accept. What offends you is Life showing you where inner focus is required.

Create awareness when anger arises today and ask yourself why it is showing up in your life.

137

Tip of the Day

"Stay out of your personal courtroom today!"

In Life, we play all the key roles in a court of law. We judge ourselves harshly. As the jury, we guilt ourselves so we are blind to our innocence. As our defense attorney, we attempt to justify what we say and how we behave. As prosecutor, we condemn ourselves to an emotionally debilitating life sentence. *Is this a courtroom where justice and love are served?*

Be open to keeping the doors to your courtroom closed today until you are willing to select a more loving type of personal justice system.

138

Tip of the Day

"Put some heart into your talent today!"

There is not a human being that does not possess at least one gift. The 'stars' or top performers in any field of endeavor are viewed as successful because they put their *heart* into whatever their talent may be. When your talent or area of expertise is not shining like you want or producing results you desire, jump start it with a dose of heart.

Toss your heart into the talent mix today.

139

Tip of the Day

"Be on the lookout for good news today!"

Affirm the statement: *'I expect to witness and receive good news today!'* By consistently saying this to yourself or out loud, you are guaranteed that surprise packages of goodness will come your way and into your life. This is an exercise in consistency of focus. Remember, what you give attention to expands; so place it on good tidings and results.

Participate in the good news today.

140

Tip of the Day

"Choose today or another day to do nothing and just 'be' with YOU!"

If possible, on this day, have no communication with others. This exercise requires commitment and fortitude because you are likely to be exposed to constant external stimulation. Occupy your day with YOU. Read a book. Take a walk in nature. Sit in silence. By just 'being,' you become aware that there is an intimate partner you have been ignoring for way too long!

Pick today or one day this week to just be with YOU.

141

Tip of the Day

"Accept everyone you come in to contact with today for who they are and what they believe!"

By living on these *terms of acceptance*, you acknowledge that everyone has the right to exist as they choose to in this life. When you find yourself trying to fix, change, convince or manipulate others, you deny them of their right to be. You also deny you your right to inner peace.

Be accepting of everyone today for their well-being and yours.

142

Tip of the Day

"Be the peace that someone else really needs today!"

The greatest act you can perform for another whose life appears challenging is to be an ambassador of peace. Your peacefulness, the energy that you emit, can have a tremendous, positive impact on another person.

Be the peace and the light that can guide someone who may be in the dark today.

143

Tip of the Day

"Be willing to ask for assistance today!"

To ask for assistance is an act of humility and courage. To believe you are less of a person by asking for help blocks you from personal and professional growth. A successful life is one that surrounds itself with people who have the intelligence and expertise to guide and support.

Be surprised by the results you get when you drop the 'I have to do it all by myself' act today.

144

Tip of the Day

"Give up being a 'drama queen' or 'drama king' today!"

Be willing to surrender your flair for the dramatics. Drama is a symptom of the need for attention (which is love). When drama is a constant presence in your life it may mean you are a drama addict. If this is the case for you, ask yourself: *"What void does this drama fill in my life?"*

Commit to not starring in dramatic roles today.

145

Tip of the Day

"Consider the consequences of your decisions today!"

Each decision you make creates a result in your life; therefore, you want to make decisions that are going to deliver who and what you want in your life. All decisions you make are rooted in how you see yourself. Know the consequences of your decisions first before you verbally respond to or act upon them.

Know the consequences you may potentially face when making a decision today.

146

Tip of the Day

"Take your cues from nature today!"

Look at the natural world and witness non-resistance and observe the acceptance of *'what is'* in any moment. There is not a plant or animal that is not connected to the process of Life. Have you ever heard an oak tree complain about the weather? Does a dog judge his master because she is having 'a bad hair day?' Look at the natural world. Notice the link between Life and amongst all life. Acknowledge your oneness with everyone and everything.

Like all creatures, be present and connected to Life today.

147

Tip of the Day

"Mind your own business today!"

Unless you are asked to assist, commit to not interfering in someone's life. Minding your own business is an exercise in self-control as well as giving up control. Everyone is on their own journey. Decide not to be the roadblock that may cause them to take unnecessary detours. In his classic 'Candide,' Voltaire wrote: "Cultivate your own garden!" This means *mind your own business!*

Concentrate on cultivating your personal plot of land that is your life today.

148

Tip of the Day

"Consider tearing up today the agreements entitled 'I will love you if...' or 'I will love you as long as you...'!

Most people treat love like a business contract. As long as the other person complies with the contract outlined in our mind, it remains binding. Any non-compliance that angers or upsets us nullifies and voids this love contract. *True love is unconditional, unsaid and unwritten.*

Consider the truth about love today.

149

Tip of the Day

"Become empowered by taking ownership of your feelings and emotions today!"

The process of owning your feelings and emotions puts you in touch with your truths and whether or not you are living life authentically. Most people ignore their feelings and emotions because they are so obsessed with how others are feeling and how others feel about them.

Develop an awareness of your feelings and emotions today so you clearly know if your life is moving in the direction you want.

150

Tip of the Day

"Starting today, change your mind about your relationship with your mind!"

Most people live life believing that the thoughts they think have no bearing on their reality. Truth be said, this is called *'mindset.'* Your mindset affects your attitude and everything else in your physical reality. Become aware that you can control your thoughts. Realize that you have the power to change your mindset and your life.

Develop a new relationship with your mind today.

151

Tip of the Day

"Use your personal history to your advantage today!"

We have a life full of stories and drama. Most times, these stories, our history, serve an unholy purpose. We tend to use our personal story to keep us victimized and stuck. If you are in the habit of using your personal history to your disadvantage be open to letting it go now! Change your perspective and know that whatever the past was you can use it to your advantage for growth and expansion. Your past does not have to equal your future. Learn from it and bless it.

Use your history to create a new game plan for all of your 'tomorrows' today.

152

Tip of the Day

"Observe yourself today and see if you withhold your 'gifts' from the world!"

We all have intellectual and creative gifts that we may not share. These gifts are our talents, and even our love. *Withholding* means we do not feel worthy of success, love or both. Ironically, we withhold what we want the most.

Notice today if you charge an exorbitant fee or withholding tax on your life and ask yourself what purpose it serves as a disservice to you.

153

Tip of the Day

"Release your grudges today!"

A grudge that you hold on to is like carrying a ball and chain. Letting go of a grudge is letting go of the past. Yesterday is history; however, do not relive or repeat it by holding on to events from the past. Grudges make you a perpetual victim. Freeing yourself of grudges liberates you from emotional pain that prevents you from seeing what is good with your life.

Be open to losing the ball and chain called grudges today.

154

Tip of the Day

"Give today what you want to receive!"

Remember this: *the world will give to you exactly what you give to it.* Decide today what it is you want from Life and simply give it where it is needed. Be it love, compassion, a friendly ear, time. No matter what it is you give, give it and it will come back to you in volumes that you could not believe possible.

Be the ultimate giver today and you will ultimately receive all you desire and more.

155

Tip of the Day

"Stop using time today as an excuse for playing small!"

We have all heard the terms using the measurement of *time* that limit, hinder and seemingly prevent us from living our lives to their full potential. *'Not enough time.' 'I am running out of time.' 'I am too old.' 'I am too young.'* These are all statements based in and about time, yet they are nothing more than excuses for living life full out now and always.

Give up time as a limitation and begin to live a grander life today.

156

Tip of the Day

"Uncover your innocence by witnessing the ways you make yourself guilty today!"

When you attack yourself for doing something 'wrong' or for not living up to unattainable standards of perfection, you leave yourself no option other than to feel guilty. When you awaken and realize that there is no 'wrong' and that perfection is your birthright, you uncover the charade you play with yourself. Once you expose the game of guilt you will see how truly innocent you are.

Discover your innocence today by not participating in the game of guilt.

157

Tip of the Day

"Take time today to focus on one unique trait, characteristic or quality you possess!"

Without exception, we each have uniqueness. No two of us are alike. What is unique about you is a bridge for you to crossover and realize *what makes you different is what makes you special.* Your specialness is the gifts you possess that can create positive change in your life and the lives of countless others.

Recognizing your uniqueness today can and will change your life and the world tomorrow.

158

Tip of the Day

"Explore your needs and desires today!"

No one and nothing can meet your needs and desires. Only you can decide and create what and who it is that fits in to your category of 'what and who do I want in my life.' Through the power of choice you can decide exactly how you want your life to unfold and what results will create true joy for you.

Knowing who and what you want today will give you clarity, focus and definition to the Being that is authentically you.

159

Tip of the Day

"Be more flexible today with yourself and others by not 'getting bent out of shape'!"

Increasing flexibility means decreasing the frequency of reactivity, over-reactivity and irritability in your life. Decide to respond rather than react. This is as easy as pausing and taking three deep breaths. Decide to come from peace, rather than negative emotions. Become aware of how impulsively you react and how easily you get emotionally upset.

Choose emotional flexibility today and witness a calmer you.

160

Tip of the Day

"Choose to be decisive today by being open to creating decisions in the moment!"

This does not mean being impulsive or 'second guessing' yourself. This requires that you pay close attention to how your heart feels when you create each and every decision. Listen to your inner voice. Begin to create a new habit of trusting yourself.

By choosing to experience and trust the process of 'in the moment decision-making' today, you will create the results you want for your life.

161

Tip of the Day

"Practice the steps necessary to being a true friend today!"

To be a true friend today be willing to 1. Show others their weaknesses, as well as their strengths, 2. Feel the fears of others, yet focus on faith, 3. Notice their anxieties, then guide them away from self-imposed worry and 4. Recognize and accept who they are today, then emphasize their limitless possibilities.

Be and do what it takes to be a true friend today.

162

Tip of the Day

"Be a leader and take people as far as they will go today!"

Many of us want people in our life to become and have what we want for them. You cannot motivate others. You can only lead by example. Know that we are all on our own journey. Lead others by being open to stretch and grow. *'Go out on a limb'* above and beyond your current level of confidence, self-worth and self-esteem. To assist others, you must be willing to go through the process yourself.

Take yourself as far as you will go today and see who follows.

163

Tip of the Day

"The fullness of life today depends on what it is lived for!"

The duration of one's life, be it long, short or somewhere in-between, is insignificant. What is significant is the *purpose* of one's life. Purpose contributes to the well-being and expansion of Life itself. Size and content of the contribution is irrelevant. Deciding to contribute is everything! Your contribution is why you are here and is your function.

Appreciate the fullness of your life today.

164

Tip of the Day

"To be joyful today, ensure that your actions are in alignment with your beliefs!"

When your activities, deeds and behavior are different from your beliefs and values, you cannot be joy-filled. Living life like this is like cutting wood against its' grain. At some point, it will crack, split and break. Create a re-alignment in your life between what you do and what you believe.

Starting today, create the necessary changes to bring more joy into your life by aligning your actions with your beliefs.

165

Tip of the Day

"Say 'out' to doubt today!"

Remove doubt from your life by focusing your faith on your unlimited potential. Doubt does nothing to enhance anyone's life. It keeps us in a world of uncertainty, stagnation, worry and fear. Doubt is turning your back on all possibilities and opportunities available to you.

Say 'out' to doubt today, even for an instant, and focus on putting the power of faith to work for you.

166

Tip of the Day

"Acknowledge your originality today!"

There is no one in this world like you. You are unique in that every aspect of your humanity and Being is one of a kind. It is at the very core of this original creation that is You, where you can discover, uncover and recover the creative talents you possess.

Know that you are an original and be proud of this fact of life today.

167

Tip of the Day

"Awaken and notice today where you are playing the game of life!"

Where do you play the game of life? Is it on a field of dreams, aspirations, certainty and wonderment? Or is it on a field of regrets, despair, uncertainty and disillusionment? Wherever you are in the game of life, promise yourself that the field you are playing on from this moment forward is home to a championship player called 'YOU!'

Play the game of life like a champion today.

168

Tip of the Day

"Realize today that personal growth is the process of becoming more of who you truly are!"

Much that has been written and said about personal growth appears to be too complicated. Personal growth is living your truth through what you feel, believe, say and do daily. Eliminate the stories (the 'untruths'). Allow who you truly are to be the dominant force in your life.

Personal growth made easy for you today.

169

Tip of the Day

"Be a messenger today!"

We are all messengers in this journey called life. Have you ever asked yourself: "What message do I have that I can share with others so they can be uplifted?" This one question could be the key that unlocks the door to a significant purpose of your life that benefits one person, many, thousands or more.

Ask yourself this potentially life-changing question and be a messenger today.

170

Tip of the Day

"Beginning today, change the way you view your life experiences!"

Most people define themselves based on their past. Know this: your experiences are not who you are. They are, however, valuable feedback in terms of who you *think* you are. Your experiences mirror back to you this belief system. Many, if not all of those beliefs you hold dear to you are not true; therefore, you are not your experiences.

Take a closer look at the relationship between you and your life experiences today.

171

Tip of the Day

"Honor yourself with kindness today!"

Acknowledging that you are your biggest critic indicates you are taking the first step toward positive change. The next step is to change the course of your emotions by bestowing kindness onto yourself. This is accepting a new role in and for your life: become a 'fan,' 'admirer' or 'advocate' for YOU.

Whatever you call it, it is about honoring yourself with kindness today.

172

Tip of the Day

"Eliminate worry from your life today!"

Worry is fear, resulting in the need to control.
All life situations fall into one of two categories.
The first is the situations we cannot control.
If you cannot control it, why worry about it?
The second category represents what we can
control. If you can control it you can create a
viable solution that leads to a desired outcome.
So, why worry about it? End of story!

Give up being a worrier today.

173

Tip of the Day

"Let people know how much you care today!"

People really do not care about how much you know; however, they do want to know how much you care. There are those around you in your life that may require extra support, assistance or guidance. Give it to them! They do not need to hear about what you know and all the 'I told you so!' responses.

Show others how much you care today and save what you know for another day.

174

Tip of the Day

"Know today that only you can motivate YOU!"

One person cannot motivate another person. There is only leading by example and inspiring. Motivation is an inside job that requires an indomitable will, perseverance and faith. To be motivated know your motivators. What excites you? What puts a smile on your face? How do you want your life to be?

The answers to these questions will position and motivate you to take action today.

175

Tip of the Day

"Play the game of life without a defense today!"

Be a science experiment today. Let down your guard and commit to NOT defending yourself no matter the circumstances or events. See what happens when you switch from defensiveness to defenselessness. You literally *'turn the other cheek'* by participating.

Notice how you feel and how your day unfolds when you play the game of life without any defense today.

176

Tip of the Day

"Practice being an example of peace today by focusing on being peaceful!"

To be this example, cease judgment and criticism. Then, commit to minding your own business. Next, stop looking for occasions to be offended. Finally, stop spreading the drama! This may seem like a tall order and it is; however, how long are you willing to live without inner peace?

You are one decision away today from the answer to inner peace.

177

Tip of the Day

"Taking one risk today can lead to one reward tomorrow!"

As children, we are told by the so-called 'experts' that life is risky business. The result is living a fear-based life where playing in the minor leagues is as major as it gets. Without risk, we cannot experience who we truly are. Taking risk is an acknowledgment of worthiness. It is telling Life that you are exposing yourself to every opportunity available to you.

By taking a risk today you are open to receiving the reward.

178

Tip of the Day

"Identify today the usual suspects that cause you emotional pain!"

What are the dominant emotions that seem to control your life? Are guilt and anger the big players? Worry, anxiety, depression? All of these suspects are disguises of fear. Ask yourself, "What is it I fear and why?" It is the question we all inevitably have to ask if we desire positive change.

Recognize your usual suspects today and begin the process of transformation.

179

Tip of the Day

"Utilize your indomitable will today!"

We are all given free will: the will to live, the will to choose, the will to move beyond so-called limitations. Be willing to move forward with courage, fortitude and focus no matter what your life situation is now.

An indomitable will today keeps you grounded; rooted in knowing that you can rise above the barriers to peace, prosperity and joy for a brighter tomorrow.

180

Tip of the Day

"Make one promise to yourself today and commit to taking it to completion!"

So often we hear the term 'broken promises' and how so many identify the story of their lives with them. In most cases, they symbolize and exemplify how frequently we say 'no' to ourselves.

Commit to one promise today for yourself and about yourself and follow it through until you create a result.

181

Tip of the Day

"To move forward today stop looking back and holding back!"

To create real, lasting, positive change in your life you must be willing to cease living in the past and holding back your gifts. These two predominant, habitual life patterns, that control most lives, can only be eliminated through the process of forgiveness.

End the habits of looking back and holding back by forgiving others and yourself today.

182

Tip of the Day

"Become conscious today of living your life one moment, one step and one day at a time!"

To live purposefully, you are required to be present as often as possible. Living 'in the now' is life-altering and life-enhancing. Without presence, you are living on auto pilot: your plane is flying without a flight course while you are asleep in the cockpit.

Practice conscious awareness by living in the moment today.

183

Tip of the Day

"Measure the immeasurable value of your personal wisdom today!"

Wisdom is inherent in all of us. It is not learned in school, talked about on the news or even discussed in casual conversation. Despite the lack of attention and airtime wisdom is given, it is big news. It is a gift we all have. When we 'turn on' our wisdom by listening to our hearts we can literally change lives, including our own.

Become aware of your wisdom today.

184

Tip of the Day

"Let go of perfectionism today!"

To always be perfect is like standing in quicksand. No matter how hard you attempt to escape, you are sunk. Perfectionism is resistance to growth and change. It is the desire to feel 'right' when you feel so 'wrong.' Realize that you are already right, already perfect as you are.

Let go of the search for perfectionism today.

185

Tip of the Day

"Be the 'silent witness' today!"

Commit to spending this day as an observer of
people, circumstances, situations and events.
Notice without judgment or analysis, what is
happening before you. Then, look below the
surface and feel what you are truly witnessing.
When you witness Life in silence you will feel one
of two aspects: love or the absence of love.

Witness your life in silence by feeling it today.

186

Tip of the Day

"Recognize today that your overall attitude is a direct result of how you see yourself?"

Negative beliefs, negative opinions, negative outlooks all create a not-so-positive attitude. They are also a result of a distortion of who you think you are. If you have a general attitude that is less than upbeat and enthusiastic it is time to assess how you rate you.

Check to see the altitude of your attitude today.

187

Tip of the Day

"Consider being paid for enjoying yourself today!"

Have you ever noticed how most people tend to omit joy and fun out of the equation when it comes to what they do for a living? Many people have adopted a false belief that compensation for money must be a miserable experience of boredom and struggle. If this is the case for you then ask yourself, "What prevents me from enjoying what I am paid for?"

Consider the joy you are missing out on today.

188

Tip of the Day

"The regrets you have regarding yesterday prevent you from living magnificently today!"

Have you ever carried a fifty pound sack of potatoes on your back? Hold that picture in your mind. Realize that is what regrets do to your body, mind and zest for life. Now, be willing to let them go once and for all. Bless them as lessons. Do not repeat them.

Move forward without the fifty pound sack of regrets today.

189

Tip of the Day

"Know the difference between being an adult and being mature today!"

Many adults have careers, marriages, children and other *'grown-up'* responsibilities. None of these roles deems a person mature. To be mature is to live without blame, judgment and participating in *'head games'* with others. It is about being brutally honest with you, behaving ethically with integrity and the best of intentions.

Notice how mature you are today.

190

Tip of the Day

"To create positive change in your life today, commit to focusing on you!"

Most people spend their lives hoping that others change so they can be happy and at peace. This never achieves the desired result because true happiness and peace can only come from within. Therefore, to create what you desire most comes from within you, too!

Focus on creating positive change from within today and witness miraculous results.

191

Tip of the Day

"Listen to your inner voice today!"

It may be a whisper, a shout or something in-between. It is the voice within you that wants you to be at peace, joy-filled and one with your Self. The voice comes from that part of you that is changeless and eternal. It wants you to achieve all your dreams and desires. Stop ignoring your inner voice. It's time to listen!

Have an open dialogue with your inner voice today.

192

Tip of the Day

"Be open-minded today!"

Open-mindedness is not just about accepting the diversity of life. It is also a state of consciousness that is demonstrated by being receptive to all the goodness available to you and for you. To be open-minded requires you to know that the supply of goodness, which consists of a variety of 'goodies,' is infinite.

Recognize the advantages to being open-minded today.

193

Tip of the Day

"Awaken to this truth today: just because certain people in your life do not love you in a way that you want, does not mean that they do not love you!"

Everyone expresses love on their own terms based on parameters they believe to be 'safe.' It does not mean there is no love. It may mean that in this moment this is the only way they can show it.

Accept and acknowledge all forms of love given to you today.

194

Tip of the Day

*"The foundation you build
for your life today determines
the shape, form and content
of your tomorrow!"*

All that you think, say and do today creates
the reality of who you will become and the
content of your life tomorrow. Decide today how
you want your life to be. Act today to create
results you want for a fulfilled tomorrow.

*Strengthen your foundation
for your life today by making
choices that stabilize and
enhance the structure that is you.*

195

Tip of the Day

"Make an agreement with yourself today to reduce and minimize complaining!"

Complaining is another form of giving our power away to other people, situations or events. It places us in the role of being a victim, playing 'small' and is emotionally exhausting. Agree to stop yourself before filing any verbal, email or text message complaints.

Feel more grounded and at peace today when you let go of the need to complain.

196

Tip of the Day

"Become clear about what you want in and for your life today!"

Most people go through life not knowing what it is they want. They are clear on what they DO NOT WANT and this becomes the subject of focus. We all have the powers of choice and focus and the ability to exercise both.

Starting today, allow you, your mind and your heart to focus on what it is you DO WANT in and for your life.

197

Tip of the Day

"To accept who you are begin the process of 'becoming comfortable in your own skin' today!"

This means no criticism and judgment typically attached to personal self-analysis. It is about being at ease, honest and at one with yourself. It does not mean better! Being comfortable in your own skin allows your authentic self to express itself and initiates a shift toward self-trust and self-acceptance.

Practice the process of being comfortable in your own skin today.

198

Tip of the Day

"Hold yourself accountable today to your commitments and contributions!"

Do not let your emotions and moods control what you do or do not do. Decide that no matter how you may be feeling today you will meet and complete your personal and professional obligations. Excuses like 'too tired,' 'too busy,' 'too overwhelmed' are not valid if you want growth in any and all areas of your life.

Be accountable to YOU today.

199

Tip of the Day

"Demonstrate one attribute you have today by putting it to use for something good!"

We each have our own unique strengths. They come in the forms of physical or mental capabilities or aspects of our character. No matter what the form, share and see the positive benefits it produces. It can have far-reaching effects. Do not underestimate your unique strength!

Overestimate your unique strengths by using them for goodness sake today.

200

Tip of the Day

"Take time today to define what makes a relationship strong!"

Often we are unclear about relationships and what makes them strong. What is important to you when it comes to relationships? Do you have unrealistic expectations or none at all? Do you have a list of conditions or none at all? Be clear about what makes a relationship strong.

Apply these attributes today to the relationships that are vital to you and watch how your relationships thrive and flourish.

201

Tip of the Day

"Learn something new about yourself today based on your encounters!"

How you interact with, relate to, communicate with and treat others reflects how you see yourself. This is based upon the feelings and beliefs you have about yourself. Do they emphasize co-operation, kindness, trust and mutual respect? If no, then ask yourself, "Why?"

Be mindful of the content of your encounters today and learn something new about yourself.

202

Tip of the Day

"Live life today like no one is watching you!"

Have you ever observed a child playing by himself? No inhibitions, editing or censoring. Just having a great time! Where is it written that adults cannot have the same experience? Being childlike is not, as many believe, being childish. A childlike quality is an asset that provides a venue for creativity to emerge.

Be childlike today and do not care if someone is watching.

203

Tip of the Day

"Be willing to participate in more mutually beneficial conversations today!"

Is there a particular relationship in your life that requires an emotional tune-up? To enliven, enhance and enrich this relationship begin a dialogue that is rich in content and meaning for both of you, rather than being superficially filled with events of the day. Deep conversation can bring you closer to anyone you choose.

Be open to participating in a dialogue that can benefit you and someone else today.

204

Tip of the Day

"Acknowledge one 'not-so-feel-good' emotion today that is present in your life!"

Begin by identifying the emotion by name. Whatever you call it, it is always fear. Ask yourself, "What is it right now that I fear?" You will receive an answer. This exercise allows you to recognize the fear and to see if it is valid. Most times it is not valid. It also begins the process of moving toward more 'feel-good' emotions.

Let go of one 'not-so-feel-good' emotion and feel good more of the time today.

205

Tip of the Day

"Be a trailblazer today!"

A trailblazer is a pioneer. A trailblazer is the first to sail on 'unchartered waters.' Trailblazing is the willingness to explore in areas you feel are important and can benefit others. Being a trailblazer is about being a leader. Do you have a cause requiring attention? Create the recognition. Do you have an idea that could change lives? Share it with someone who is supportive, admirable and trust-worthy. Take action. Deal with challenges as they arise.

Be a trailblazer today.

206

Tip of the Day

"Give up playing roles today and become a role model for living an extraordinary life!"

We all have fallen into the trap of pigeon-holed roles: wife, husband, mother, father, boss, employee, etc. Each role has what we think are exemplary traits to aspire to. As we seek to perfect our roles we can easily forget how to experience a fulfilling life.

Drop the roles today and simply be a role model for living a full, rich and rewarding life.

207

Tip of the Day

"The mistakes you make today do not define who you are!"

The biggest misconception we have about ourselves is we confuse our behavior with our 'Self.' We equate making a mistake with being less than worthy. Mistakes are something you do, they are not who you are. Failure to create a desired result does not make you a failure.

Remember today that you make mistakes... mistakes do not make you.

208

Tip of the Day

"Let people know you respect them today!"

It is important to express good feelings toward others. When you truly feel good about someone tell them. Expressing respect has huge benefits. First, it uplifts the receiver of the compliment. Second, as the giver, you are being real and reducing your inhibition to express feelings. Third, you are building strong, genuine relationships.

Tell someone you respect them today.

209

Tip of the Day

"Focus on teamwork today!"

Teamwork, both professionally and at home with family members, is harmonious cooperation. This means that there is a willingness to voluntarily be a team player. With the spirit of teamwork, success is guaranteed. Add harmony and cooperation to wherever you are and you create environments that are ripe for prosperity.

Focus on teamwork by being a key player today.

210

Tip of the Day

"Develop a more self-reliant attitude today!"

Take responsibility for your own life and your emotional needs. Self-reliance also includes the understanding that a certain number of people may dislike or disapprove of you. Nevertheless, a self-reliant attitude gives love, approval, acceptance and understanding to other people. The result is a receiving of the same.

Become more self-reliant today.

211

Tip of the Day

"Create a more success-oriented personality today by having more interest in and regard for other people!"

Truly successful people respect the challenges and needs of others. Respect the dignity of people as human beings and not as a means toward an end. This charitable approach creates a deeper level of respect and regard you have for yourself.

Care about others today and develop a more success-oriented 'YOU.'

212

Tip of the Day

"To make a good impression today, do not try to consciously make a good impression!"

To accomplish this, give up monitoring every word, action or mannerism. Allow your creative self to emerge. Stop worrying about what others think or say about you. When you come from your heart, you are who you truly are. The result is a good impression, first, second or otherwise.

To make a good impression just be YOU today.

213

Tip of the Day

"Put some distance between you and your challenges today!"

By temporarily walking away from your challenges you allow yourself to view them from a different perspective. A new perspective can provide you with more breathing room. It can also give you the space to create solutions.

Create more distance between you and your challenges today and watch how a change in scenery can positively change your life.

214

Tip of the Day

"Tap into your imagination today!"

The gift of imagination is an integral part of the evolution process of humankind. We all possess the capacity to imagine, yet for most it is greatly under-utilized. Make the most of your imagination. It is the field where the seeds of your creativity can germinate into life changing ideas for you and others. Imagination is a resource with a limitless supply.

Be open to using your imagination today.

215

Tip of the Day

"Be of 'good cheer' today!"

To be of *'good cheer'* means to see goodness in every person, experience or situation. Be the optimist today. Focus on what is right with the world. Believe that life is good and that goodness is limitless.

Spread the cheer with a smile, a gesture, a deed or your positive energy today.

216

Tip of the Day

"Acknowledge today that you are an original, one-of-a-kind creation!"

There is no one else exactly like you. Never has and never will there be anyone with your combination of talent, creativity, skill and know-how. Take that uniqueness with all its assets and make the most of it for yourself and others.

Capitalize on being an original work of art and allow the masterpiece that is YOU feel appreciated by everyone today.

217

Tip of the Day

"Set your emotional thermostat to the 'calm and relaxed' zone today!"

Our bodies have a built-in thermostat keeping our temperature at 98.6F no matter what the temperature around us is. Likewise, you can set your emotional state at peaceful even if the emotional weather around you is not. Take a deep breath, count to ten before responding and stay present.

Set your emotional thermostat to the 'calm and relaxed' zone today.

218

Tip of the Day

"Commit to eliminating excuses as part of your daily routine today!"

Excuses are postponements. Excuses are deflections of responsibility and are 'escape routes' for the immature. Excuses deplete your personal power. Decide to be mature and accept responsibility for your participation or lack thereof in any situation you consented to be part of.

Starting today, commit to stop making excuses for you and others.

219

Tip of the Day

"Stop seeking love today!"

Instead of looking for love focus on identifying the barriers you put up to prevent love from entering your life. To receive love you must be open to it. You have to feel deserving of the experience love offers. Once you identify these barriers ask yourself why you erected them. Then, when you are ready to remove them, you will be amazed to learn that you know longer have to seek love.

Stop seeking love today by removing the barriers to experiencing it and see how quickly love finds you.

220

Tip of the Day

"Know today that the world needs you now!"

You and your life are significant. Your contribution to the well-being of the world is without question. It is irrefutable! The very fact that you exist implies a unique purpose. To know what that purpose is and what form it takes can only be determined by your acknowledgment that your role is important.

Accept the truth that you are important to you and your world today.

221

Tip of the Day

"Be a visionary today!"

We all have the ability to visualize. We also have the ability to choose the content of our visions. Begin a new phase, a new era for your life by envisioning how you want your life to be from this day forward. Know that you are just one vision away from changing your life and potentially the lives of countless others.

Believe your visions can become reality today and witness their appearances tomorrow.

222

Tip of the Day

"Realize today that true success for you comes from your heart!"

When you listen to your heart you are hearing your truth. Your truth, whatever form or substance it may be, is what success is for you. Truly successful results in life emanate from feeling success-filled first. The only way to experience this process is to live in and from your heart.

From today forward, know that your true success resides in your heart.

223

Tip of the Day

"Positive changes in your life today are measured by your willingness to take the next step!"

Growth on any level is not measured by the number of or size of the steps you take. The greatest catalyst for change is simply a decision and willingness to create it. Once that decision is made guidance appears in ways you may not even be able to conceive.

Be willing to take a step toward positive change today.

224

Tip of the Day

"Add value to the people in your life today!"

Everyone desires to be appreciated. However, when you believe certain people are hindering or blocking your happiness or success you will likely use deception, manipulation and control to get what you desire. Instead, consciously choose to show others how much you appreciate them.

Create an attitude of mutual admiration today by seeing and acknowledging the value of the people in your life.

225

Tip of the Day

"Live without limits today!"

All limitations are self-imposed. Self-imposed limitations contain two acts of injustice. First, we deny our infinite nature backed by our capacities to be limitless creators and second, we live from a perspective of selfishness by withholding from others the potential we all possess for creating growth and change.

Be just to yourself and the world today by deciding to live without limits.

226

Tip of the Day

"Become familiar with your convictions today!"

A conviction is simply a strong belief. What and who do you strongly believe in? Does the life you are living reflect those beliefs? Living life based on convictions is called being 'grounded.' Create a list of what and who you strongly believe in. Notice if who you are and how you are living are in alignment with those beliefs.

Identify your convictions today.

227

Tip of the Day

"Lighten up about life today!"

Most of us take life way too seriously. Being serious most of the time has some 'serious' implications. Seriousness implies an attitude of doom and gloom. It reflects an inability to experience joy. Change your focus and see that life is mostly humorous. Begin to laugh off so-called serious situations and events.

Lighten up and lighten your 'load' by being less serious today.

228

Tip of the Day

"Speed up the process of positive change by becoming more open to learning today!"

When we believe we 'know it all' and are always right we cannot evolve and grow. Learning implies expansion. To learn more, be open to new ideas. Listen more, observe more and talk less. Speed up the learning process by asking questions and for guidance.

Use these suggestions and see how learning positively affects your life today.

229

Tip of the Day

"Borrow from the future today!"

The future is a sequence of events that has not occurred yet; however, is available for you exclusively now. The future is like a trust account that you can withdraw from to create whatever it is your heart desires. Think, see, feel and acting in accord with how you want your life to be right here and now. This is the process of borrowing from the future.

Live a bright future by borrowing from it today.

230

Tip of the Day

"Seek commonality today!"

We are so conditioned to point out the differences between ourselves and others. We are quick to identify and criticize behaviors, habits and lifestyles of people we know and more often, do not know. Why not shift your perspective by noticing what you have in common with others? For starters, how about the universal need to be loved and accepted?

Notice today how much we all have in common.

231

Tip of the Day

"*Make a new connection today!*"

A key aspect of creating success in life is building relationships. To create new relationships you have to be willing to 'put yourself out there' where people gather, exchange ideas, create, inspire and guide. One new connection can literally change the course of your life.

Make yourself available to connecting with new people today and create new possibilities for tomorrow.

232

Tip of the Day

"Take time today to identify the key factors in your life that you are absolutely UNWILLING to change!"

Feel how solid the ground you walk on is by knowing what you are unwilling to change or compromise in your life. This may include your faith, integrity, compassion, confidence, self-respect and self-esteem to name a few.

Recognize your unchangeable factors as sources of great power that keep the spirit in you thriving today.

233

Tip of the Day

"Starting today, choose your friends wisely!"

Many people seem to have 'lots of friends' because of their need for acceptance. Friendship is measured by quality, not quantity. A true friend lifts you up when you feel down. A friend does not judge or criticize, yet confronts you when you act inappropriately. A friend is present during the good times and the lean.

Establish your parameters for authentic friendship today.

234

Tip of the Day

"Whatever you hold onto today may be holding you back from a brighter tomorrow!"

A grudge, an unhealthy relationship, a skill or talent you are reluctant to share. 'Holding on' is living a life of stagnation and indignation. You deny yourself and others the ability to experience joy. It cuts off the flow of life. It is like being a hoarder. Be open to releasing that which no longer serves you.

Let go today of beliefs, behaviors, people and possessions that no longer serve you.

235

Tip of the Day

"Rather than seeking your life's purpose, live 'on purpose' today!"

To live your life 'on purpose' means you are giving your all to everything you do. 'On purpose' is the process of immersing yourself with the gifts, talents, know-hows you possess, into your daily routine. You can never know your purpose unless you align your whole being with living 'on purpose.'

Live your life 'on purpose' today.

236

Tip of the Day

"Determine what kind of influence you exert on others today!"

Influence is energy. How do you use yours? Is it encouraging and uplifting or do you find yourself needing to control people? Do you seek to make you look bigger and better by deliberately making others feel small? Are you leading by success-oriented examples or are you seeking to make yourself 'look good'?

Identify the energy you exert today and where needed, adjust those intentions to being a positive influence and an example for positive change.

237

Tip of the Day

"Know the importance of having integrity today!"

Integrity is the greatest asset you can possess if you seek respect and desire to be viewed as trustworthy. Act out of integrity and you behave in alignment with who you are at the center of your being. You live by a set of principles that exemplifies a grounded character. A person of integrity is a person of positive influence.

Consciously act out of integrity in all that you are, say and do today.

238

Tip of the Day

"Expand your relationship circle today!"

In relationships, we tend to gravitate toward people with likes, interests and backgrounds similar to our own. The drawback to this approach is that it limits personal growth, the exchange of diverse experiences, knowledge and creativity.

Increase the size of your relationship circle today by diversifying and expanding who you are willing to meet and get to know.

239

Tip of the Day

"Be willing to give up using a 'handicap' today as an excuse for not living an extraordinary life!"

Reflect on these extraordinary lives: Helen Keller, U.S. President Franklin D. Roosevelt, Physicist Stephen Hawking, actors Christopher Reeve and Michael J. Fox. Open yourself up to releasing so-called physical, mental or financial deficiencies such as: not pretty, smart or rich enough as reasons for not living life to its full capacity.

Drop the idea of using 'handicaps' as your excuse today.

240

Tip of the Day

"Add value today to the person who is YOU by identifying the aspects of who you are that could benefit from coaching and personal development!"

Memorize this statement: 'You cannot give what you do not have.' To be more loving, love yourself more. To be kinder, add kindness to your life. To be giving, add generosity to your daily routine. To be more, add more of what you want. This can be accomplished by adding coaching and personal development into your life.

Be more today by adding value to the 'who' that is YOU.

241

Tip of the Day

"Overlook the petty, unimportant and mundane today!"

How much energy and time in your day do you give to 'non-productivity?' This includes people, events and activities that keep you from creating the success results you desire. To move beyond the 'non-productive,' it is essential to prioritize who and what are important to you and why.

Focus on the productive aspects of your life today.

242

Tip of the Day

"Expand your creative power today!"

To expand your creative horizons it is important to know that your mind has limitless capabilities. To unleash this creative force within you, be willing to release yourself from the ball and chain known as self-criticism. Give yourself permission to being open to new avenues of self-expression.

Explore the infinite Universe that is YOU today and see what you discover.

243

Tip of the Day

"Know the direction you are being pulled toward today!"

We are always heading somewhere either physically or emotionally. It is important to become aware of where you are being pulled and the type of energy that is pulling you. The easiest way to uncover this is to recognize how you are feeling. If you feel good, stay the course. If you do not, stop and look within for guidance.

Where are you heading today?

244

Tip of the Day

"Keep your eyes open today!"

Most people walk through life with 'blinders' on. When you wear blinders you allow Life's gifts to pass you by. In reality, all of Life's gifts are yours for the taking. The experience that is Life is composed of love, joy, beauty, appreciation, limitless possibilities and opportunities. Enjoy the fruits of Life, remove the 'blinders' and be present to receive.

Keep your eyes open to see what Life has to offer you today.

245

Tip of the Day

"Bless wherever you are on your life's journey today!"

Too often people express dissatisfaction for their current life and current situations. They are convinced that they 'should be further along' for a person of their age, experience or education. Know this: you are exactly where you are divinely intended to be in any given moment. And how do you know this? Because, *you are where you are!* Accept this as truth to create change.

Be grateful for today and the life that is you.

246

Tip of the Day

"Become acquainted with your personal life philosophy today!"

We all have our own philosophy of and about life. This is best illustrated by how we see ourselves, the world and how we choose to live our lives according to our beliefs. Do you like what you see? If not, check your philosophy. Make adjustments by creating a new philosophy. This can dramatically change your life.

Get to know your life philosophy today.

247

Tip of the Day

"Consider the possibility today that all successes in life are spiritual in nature!"

Success is categorized: financial, career, relationships, health. A lack of success in any area is the result of a spiritual discord or how you feel about you! Any area of your life that feels less than gratifying has a spiritual lesson built in to it. Observe positive change by looking within for solutions.

Choose a spiritually successful life today.

248

Tip of the Day

"The measure of who you are today is determined by the level of humanity you choose to live at!"

Your humanity is composed of the desirable qualities that are YOU. Humanity is the quality of being humane. To be humane requires kindness, mercy and knowing the appropriate response to any event, situation or experience.

Consciously measure yourself today and if necessary, raise your level of humanity.

249

Tip of the Day

"Starting today, become a 'Yes, I can' and a 'Yes, I am' person!"

Notice the frequency of the words 'can't' and 'not' in your vocabulary and when they are used to describe you and your so-called inability to achieve the results you want. Even if it feels strange at first, 'flip the switch' and affirm 'I can...' and 'I am...' Complete these phrases with words that allow you to feel good and shine inside and out.

Become a 'Yes' person who says 'Yes' to Life today.

250

Tip of the Day

"Add something extra to an ordinary experience today!"

When you give something extra you instantly turn your focus onto all that is good. Something extra can appear to be ordinary: a smile, greeting someone or letting another person know you care. You can also add enthusiasm to your tasks and change the dynamics of how you feel. You will see improved results, too.

Put something extra into your day today.

251

Tip of the Day

"Where you are today is the result of your best thinking!"

Your life in this moment is a direct effect of all your yesterdays. Do you like your current state of affairs? If not, create changes by changing your thinking. Thoughts create things. There is no exception to this rule. The good news is you can freely adjust and change your thought patterns so tomorrow is different than today.

Ensure that your thinking today is creating the best tomorrow for you.

252

Tip of the Day

"Who is steering your ship today?"

Are you the number one decision maker when it comes to the direction your life is heading toward? Or, do you allow others to influence you to sail in undesirable waters? Steering your ship is an image for empowerment. When you are at the helm you choose the course you desire to sail. Take over the wheel! YOU are the captain of your ship!

Be self-assured, take the wheel and steer your ship today.

253

Tip of the Day

"Every desire you feel today is a desire to feel good!"

Desire is a natural gift unique to humans. Rooted in desire is a desire to feel good. All we truly want is to feel the peace that permeates all life. The exception to this is intentions to harm another person or any life form. These are reactions to inner conflict, not desires.

Act on one desire today to create a feeling of goodness and inner peace.

254

Tip of the Day

"Keep on loving today!"

No matter how your day evolves, focus on the power of love. Even if you are feeling down and out for the count, know that love and being loving is the only way to rise above any situation. When tomorrow comes, the current events of your life will be fleeting memories of the past.

Surround your current circumstances and yourself with love today.

255

Tip of the Day

"Make today a special occasion by acknowledging it as a unique opportunity for creating positive results!"

Each day that we have is only as special as we decide it can be. The absolute truth is that every day possesses a specialness all its own. Acknowledge today as special and unique. Anticipate wonderful events to unfold before you. See yourself as the receiver of good news.

Expect goodness and marvel how special an occasion today really is.

256

Tip of the Day

"Step back today if it feels challenging to move forward!"

Stepping back from a difficult situation or relationship does not mean you have resolved to quitting or giving up. Stepping back allows you create physical and emotional distance. It can provide you with a fresh and renewed perspective in a way you may have never thought possible.

Step back today so you can move forward tomorrow.

257

Tip of the Day

"Allow yourself to receive the answers today!"

To obtain answers you must first become aware of the questions. What questions have you been seeking answers to, yet are not getting a response? Within you are all the answers to your questions. The only barrier that stands between you and the answers you seek is YOU!

Step aside, relax, ask a question, and see the answer appear today.

258

Tip of the Day

"Create changes in your life today by taking inventory of your natural resources!"

Your natural resources are gifts and talents that are a unique product line manufactured by YOU. Are your products sitting on a shelf collecting dust waiting for their expiration date? Create an inventory checklist. Ask yourself, "How can the products that are my unique gifts and talents be shared with the world?"

Identify your natural resources today.

259

Tip of the Day

"Support your personal causes today!"

Your personal causes are your dreams, ideas and creations that you know can enrich your life and the lives of countless others. Stop denying these causes! They have sat on the 'back burner' far too long. Do not expect support from others if you are unwilling to give it to yourself.

Witness how your life dramatically improves when you support YOU and your causes today.

260

Tip of the Day

"Create a new viewpoint regarding conflict today!"

Believe it or not, conflict in your life is a blessing. When you experience conflict you are in a position of opportunity for growth. You are being shown an aspect of your life that requires healing. Your willingness to heal determines if the conflict continues or dissipates. Notice the presence of conflict in your life.

Choose one current conflict in your life and ask yourself how it may be today's blessing.

261

Tip of the Day

"Allow stumbling blocks to inspire and invigorate you today!"

Changing your viewpoint toward so-called stumbling blocks and barriers to success and happiness can have a profound effect on the results you experience in this lifetime. See stumbling blocks as opportunities and you put yourself in a position to create positive change.

Be inspired and energized if you encounter a stumbling block today.

262

Tip of the Day

"Acknowledge how your goodness contributes to the lives of others!"

We all play key roles in the process called Life; however, many of us minimize our contributions and our capacity to make a difference in the lives of other people. Does this describe you? If yes, then now is the time to recognize that there is so much goodness residing within you.

Give yourself permission to put your goodness to use today.

263

Tip of the Day

"Give attention today to the one area of your life that you have been neglecting for too long!"

Life happens! We move at warp speed. In the process, aspects of our life show signs of neglect and atrophy. It could be your mind, your body or your relationships. Identify the imbalance in your life and create a shift in energy. The result is a better-feeling you.

Pay attention to a 'neglected' part of you today.

264

Tip of the Day

"As you seek respect from others today, make sure you put the word 'mutual' first!"

Everyone expects respect; however, most who expect have difficulty giving it. The act of giving respect is not intended to be based on pre-existing conditions. Respect is a quality of the spirit that has no boundaries, plays no favorites and seeks nothing in return.

Live the purest form of respect today by making it mutual.

265

Tip of the Day

"Discover today what motivates you to take inspired action!"

We each have what are called *'motivation factors.'* These are desires, visions and situations that propel us to create on behalf of ourselves and of others. They are what *'rocks your boat.'* If you are experiencing a lack of inspiration then you have lost sight of your *'motivation factors.'*

Gain clarity today by identifying what 'rocks your boat.'

266

Tip of the Day

"Your success today depends on the success of others!"

True success of any kind is a team effort. Live your life as a collaborative effort and less of a competition to survive. There are so many diverse forms of prosperity and abundance so everyone can enjoy the journey of success.

Collaborating with others to create mutually beneficial outcomes is the most effective approach to achieving results today.

267

Tip of the Day

"Drop the 'superiority complex' today!"

Any belief or feeling you have that indicates you are better than anyone else will always bring less than satisfying outcomes. The need to outdo, outshine and outlast will sooner or later lead you to a very solitary existence. Recognize yourself from within.

Realize the only approval you require is your own and watch your 'superiority complex' fade away today.

268

Tip of the Day

"Receive a new perspective today about yourself?"

Ask a member of your *'personal fan club':* a friend, co-worker, loved one, to describe who they see and what they feel when it comes to you. Others see us so differently than we see ourselves. A new perspective can shine the light on untapped traits, characteristics and attributes.

Let a member of your fan club describe how they see and feel about you today.

269

Tip of the Day

"Be open and willing to let go of the need to control today!"

Are you someone who is so wound up all the time because they need to control and manipulate people and situations in their life so they can be at peace? It may take courage to admit it; however, if this describes you, then you are really out-of-control. To be controlling is a symptom of fear and a lack of trust. Ask yourself, "What am I afraid of and why do I have an untrusting nature about people and situations in my life?"

Examine your tendencies to control today and notice how you prevent yourself from living in peace.

270

Tip of the Day

"Consider today that you have one relationship with many people!"

You may believe that you have many relationships with many people. The truth is the relationships you have with other people are an extension of the relationship you have with yourself. Any disharmony and discord you have with other people dissolves as you change from within.

Be open to looking at the one and only relationship in your life today.

271

Tip of the Day

"Find a cause that you are passionate about today!"

Each of us has a purpose, even multiple purposes that come and go, and vary in focus and intensity during one's lifetime. Within you exists a spark that is ignited by something outside of you. A cause is the stage where you can express what you believe in and feel strongly about.

Find a cause today and you have chosen a purpose to call your own.

272

Tip of the Day

"Use your personal encounter with failure wisely today!"

Despite what you may or may not believe about experiencing failure, realize this: it is never fatal! Failure is simply a message stating 'create a different approach to obtain your desired result.' Failure also gives you a tremendous appreciation for your successes.

Use failure as your stepping-stone to creating success today.

273

Tip of the Day

"Be willing to measure your personal progress today!"

Progress is a forward movement. It is about staying on a path of development. Whichever aspect of your life you are currently seeking to enrich, be open to acknowledging your progress. By knowing where you are, and where you were yesterday, you gain clarity on where you can be tomorrow. You will now possess what it takes to get you where you want to be.

Measure your progress today.

274

Tip of the Day

"The rapid pace of change in your world requires having more faith in yourself today!"

Our world is changing in so many ways and at such a rapid pace, that it is so easy to lose sight and touch with ourselves. There is one constant; however, that is changeless: who you are at your core or the spiritual you. This is where it is essential to place your faith and remain grounded no matter what is going on around you.

Keep the faith from within today and know the changeless YOU in an ever-changing world.

275

Tip of the Day

"Commit to being total love today!"

To be total love requires you to be present, living in the 'now.' It means you are open, honest and transparent. You are willing to express the love in your heart fully. To be total love requires you to be emotionally 'naked' without hidden agendas or motives.

Commit to seeing a glimpse of being a loving person today and you will experience life with the real you.

276

Tip of the Day

"Let your sixth sense guide you to being successful today!"

We all possess a sixth sense or extra sensory perception, yet many of us neglect using this gift. Making the most of the sixth sense requires listening to your heart and knowing that it will steer you toward happy situations and outcomes. This requires trusting your inner voice, your heart and most of all your natural instincts.

Let your sixth sense be your guide today.

277

Tip of the Day

"Use your personal preferences today to create positive changes!"

Rather than living from the position based on who you think you are, begin to live from a position of who you want to be. Living from a place of who you think you are keeps you in the past. When you shift your preferences to being the result of positive changes you desire, you create a different future.

Become who you desire to be today.

278

Tip of the Day

"Be willing to listen to and apply one piece of advice from someone you admire and respect today!"

Too often, we are closed off from accepting guidance from others. We believe it is a sign of weakness and being less than adequate to achieve whatever it is we seek to accomplish. Know that no success is ever created as a 'one man' or 'one woman' show.

Accepting one piece of advice today from someone you look up to can change your life tomorrow.

279

Tip of the Day

"Make a lasting impression today!"

Have you ever created a memory for someone else? A time when you went beyond what was expected of you? Can you recall a special, glorious time in someone else's life that you masterminded? A lasting impression can have life-changing consequences.

Consider someone in your life who could benefit today from a memory created by one of your lasting impressions.

280

Tip of the Day

"There are no limitations to what you can achieve today!"

Most people, by the time they are young adults, have convinced themselves that they possess unlimited limitations. The prevailing thought and belief of these 'limitations' is some form of 'I am not enough!' All limitations are self-imposed.

Be willing to put these limiting thoughts and beliefs to the test today and see how valid or invalid they are.

281

Tip of the Day

"Producing a result quickly today does not guarantee success!"

In our hyperactive world *'get it done yesterday'* has become the mantra. A fast result is not always the desired result. When you do not *feel* the process of success, you are likely moving too fast. A successful result requires productive action; however, it also requires nurturing, planning and intuition.

Slow down today and feel the process of success.

282

Tip of the Day

"Improve your emotional health today by acknowledging your feelings regarding an unresolved issue in your life!"

Holding unexpressed or unrecognized feelings will result in extreme emotional discord. You literally stuff down the truth that is YOU. This is a signal to you that it is time to address and bring to the surface feelings you are holding onto. This is how we heal and reconnect with our true selves.

Be open and willing to acknowledge what you feel today.

283

Tip of the Day

"Take time today to know the 'teachers' in your life!"

There are aspects of your life that you see as problems. They show up repeatedly in many forms: stress, chaos, people, illnesses and drama, keeping you in a state of unrest. These 'problems' are a higher power communicating with you to rise above any situation and move forward with your life.

Look at your 'problems' today and consider the possibility they may be your best 'teachers.'

284

Tip of the Day

"Be a 'contributing factor' on the road of success for you and all the teams you play for today!"

Most people equate success with gains and achievements; however, true success requires real contribution and creativity as a team. Contribution requires commitment, focus, purpose and a willingness to give for the highest good of all. The level of contribution determines the results of all collaborations and team work.

Be a 'contributing factor' for you and everyone in your life today.

285

Tip of the Day

"Do not let your emotions control or paralyze you today!"

Do you allow your emotions to dictate your behavior? When they do, you are giving your power away to a habit that is typically fed by reactivity and irrational responses. Realize that you can control your emotions. You do have that choice. Notice who and what causes your emotions to overpower you.

Take charge of your emotions today.

286

Tip of the Day

"Know the basic requirements for living your life's purpose today!"

True purpose is about giving unconditionally and being grateful for what you receive in return. The result of living *'on purpose'* may not be the result you envisioned. Accept that possibility. Nothing will be given to you that you cannot handle or do not need.

Enter the realm of purposeful living and experience a richer life today.

287

Tip of the Day

"Be open to improving your social skills today!"

In our world of techno-overload, the art of verbal communication is rapidly becoming extinct. Now, more than ever, the art of mastering interpersonal relationships is an essential talent for creating true success both personally and professionally. Let others know what your voice sounds like. Go back to the basics. Engage in conversations. Listen to another person. Connect eye ball to eye ball.

Put down and shut down the technology and jump start your social skills today.

288

Tip of the Day

"Perform an emotional audit today and see if you are overspending on your 'defense budget'!"

Are you on the defensive expecting arguments, defending yourself, or being on guard for a negative situation? Overspending your personal defense budget depletes your emotional resources. You waste time, energy and empty your *'inner peace account.'* It may be time to curtail your defense spending.

Do an emotional audit today and decide whether or not you want to decrease your defense budget.

289

Tip of the Day

"Understand the powerful function of relationships today!"

Most people complain that the majority of their relationships are challenging at best. These very same people miss knowing the true function of all relationships. Relationships are tools for creating, healing and learning. On the deepest level, all relationships are divinely given. Despite appearances and in spite of circumstances surrounding them, relationships are blessings.

Enjoy the benefits of your relationships today by acknowledging what you are receiving from each and every one of them.

290

Tip of the Day

"Be willing to say what you really feel today!"

Do you say 'yes' when you really mean 'no'? Do you say 'no' when you really mean 'yes'? Or are you an always 'maybe' kind of person? Perhaps you are being a 'people pleaser;' someone who tries to be all things to all people.

Instead of giving lip service to satisfy others, stand your ground and say what you feel today.

291

Tip of the Day

"Acknowledge the absolute and irrefutable facts of your life today!"

Do the stories you tell yourself accurately depict your reality? Does how you see yourself resemble how others see you? Any difference in how you and others perceive you are a message that you may very well be living in what Einstein called an *'optical delusion.'*

Be willing to question the accuracy about the story you tell yourself about you today.

292

Tip of the Day

"Take a walk in the field of all possibilities today!"

To truly live life to its full potential is to know limitless possibility. This means being carefree about everything in life and that includes money. This does not imply being frivolous or irresponsible with financial wealth. It does imply a willingness to acknowledge and expect your share of the infinite diversity of Life that awaits you.

Enjoy your walk in the field of all possibilities today.

293

Tip of the Day

"Become a spiritual entrepreneur today!"

There is a term in economics called *'the law of supply and demand.'* Whatever gifts and talents you have to share or services and products you have to give, know there is always a level of demand for them. Ask yourself, "How may I be of service?" The answers are absolutely within you. To gain clarity, all you need do is listen. By uncovering the answers, you recognize the demand for your service.

Earn your degree in Spiritual Economics today.

294

Tip of the Day

"Consider uncovering the potential barriers to love today!"

There are three barriers that can ultimately prevent you from truly feeling loved and loving. They are neediness, jealousy and expectations. These barriers represent feelings of unworthiness, low self-esteem and believing we are flawed. Recognize these blocks to love. If they are present in your life be open to understanding how these feelings arose.

Begin the process of moving toward knowing true love today by being open to seeing if and why any of the three barriers to love are present in your life.

295

Tip of the Day

"Review any 'unfinished business' you have been neglecting today!"

Unfinished business is any emotional baggage you are carrying with you that is linked to the past. Refusing to emotionally close the door, move on, move out and put it all behind you blocks any good, joy, peace and happiness in your life. There is no time limit or statute of limitations to completing and releasing the past.

Notice any 'unfinished business' in your life today.

296

Tip of the Day

"Empower yourself today by not allowing 'small-minded' people to hold you back!"

There may be people in your life that say they know what is 'best' for you. There are others who give free advice and warn you about risk. Here are two ways to move away from the influence of negative-focused people. First and foremost, listen to your heart. Second, take advice from successful people whose life and mindset you aspire to live and be like.

Be powerful by being the creator of your life today.

297

Tip of the Day

"Realize that happiness can come from many sources and directions today!"

People tend to fixate on the idea that happiness comes from one source or direction. This is best explained with the belief 'I will be happy when...' This places conditions on happiness. When you meet one condition, a new one will emerge.

Examine your conditions for happiness today and unconditionally notice how happy you can feel.

298

Tip of the Day

"Focus on new beginnings today!"

Truly experiencing being human requires us to live in the present moment. Each moment represents a choice we always have to focus on our intentions and ultimately the results we desire. When you decide to live in the 'now' you can turn your life around and place yourself in the space of infinite potential. Be willing to let go of all thoughts, feelings and regrets of the past.

Create the results you desire by focusing on new beginnings today.

299

Tip of the Day

"Treat today and all of your experiences as a series of special events!"

Most people are conditioned for the boring and mundane as the daily norm. Life's moments can be special when we treat them that way. By giving total effort, being creative and listening to others, you can transform an ordinary day into a series of special experiences.

Commit to treating the events of this day as something special today.

300

Tip of the Day

"Rise above 'playing small' today by playing in the 'big leagues'!"

To play in the big leagues of life requires more than talent. It means you choose to release *'small'* thoughts and beliefs about yourself, not argue over small things or cry over small hurts. To play big means letting go of the petty, trivial, childish events that occur. Rise up!

Qualify yourself for playing in the 'big leagues' today.

301

Tip of the Day

"Don't be fooled by the concept of 'keeping busy' today!"

Most people mistake a list of activities for productivity and achievement. Everyone appears to be busy and that may include you. Ask yourself, "What keeps me so busy and is it giving me the results I want for my life?" Learn how to differentiate between chaos and focus.

Focus on achieving results rather than the misdirected, chaotic concept of 'keeping busy' today.

302

Tip of the Day

"Your relationship with money today is a direct reflection of your relationship with yourself?"

Financial struggle is never about the money.
This relationship is at the level of consciousness,
not how much is in your bank account.
When we feel less than whole, unworthy or
undeserving, we may face financial challenges.

Examine the relationship of your financial status and how you feel about you today.

303

Tip of the Day

"Discover today how identified you are with the roles you play!"

Role assignments are undoubtedly an integral part of the world we live in; however, the roles we play are not who we are at our core. Over-identification with a particular role and believing you are not at peak performance in that role can cause much confusion and unhappiness. You are so much more than the roles you play on a daily basis.

Ask yourself, 'Who am I?' today and see how the roles you play impact your response.

304

Tip of the Day

"Know where the true YOU resides today and every day!"

The true you, along with the world you live in, can only exist in the present moment. Experiencing Life to its' fullest can only occur *now*. This begins with practicing mindfulness. Mindfulness is awareness. It is being in touch with you at the deepest level. With practice, this becomes a way of life.

Become aware of and locate the true YOU today.

305

Tip of the Day

"Identify today the dominant attitudes in your life!"

Your attitude represents your approach and perception toward life and life's situations. Becoming aware of the attitudes that dominate your thinking provide you with an ability to control your actions and behavior. Decide not to react to your negative attitudes. Create positive attitudes by letting go of negative emotions. Give yourself permission to take positive action.

Take time out today for identifying and changing your attitudes.

306

Tip of the Day

"Be it today or any day, you only have this moment to be truly alive!"

Life does not exist in past or future. Life exists *now*. Now is an acronym for *Newness, Openness and Willingness.* Living in the *now*, being present, allows you to experience the newness of each moment. Back this by openness and willingness to experience life fully and you are well on your way to feeling on purpose and complete.

Memorize the acronym for 'now' today and witness subtle yet powerful changes.

307

Tip of the Day

"Under promise and over deliver today!"

Make commitments; however, do not 'bite off' what you know you cannot or are not willing to handle. As you proceed and find that desired results come easy, surprise yourself and others by over-delivering on promises. Committing from this position benefits you and strengthens your relationships. Ease up on promises you cannot keep.

Over deliver the 'goods' you have to give today.

308

Tip of the Day

"Recognize your strengths and weaknesses today!"

To accept 'you' in any moment is the one and only way to accept other people. First, look at yourself and identify the good, admirable and extraordinary aspects. Then, identify aspects of you that may require positive change. Recognizing the entirety that is 'you' allows you to accept yourself and ultimately others.

Be open to acknowledging your strengths and weaknesses today.

309

Tip of the Day

"Consider the possibility today that what you want most may also be what you fear!"

You want the relationship, the money, the career, etc.; however, this all comes with responsibilities. Fear of responsibility can push away what you want. Ask yourself, "Do I fear that which I want because of responsibility?"

If you answered 'yes,' then say: "I can handle any level of responsibility required of me today."

310

Tip of the Day

"Pay close attention to what you give your attention to today!"

Become aware of what and who you focus your thoughts upon. When you find yourself giving attention in a wandering, chaotic and haphazard fashion you will be unable to be fully productive. This is why people complain about their days ending without completing what they intended to do. You decide where and what your mind gives its' attention to.

Focus attention on, and if necessary change what you give attention to today.

311

Tip of the Day

"Only refer to the past today if it reflects a fond or happy memory!"

We know the term 'letting go of the past.' Shakespeare said it best when he wrote: "What's done is done!" However, reminding ourselves of positive experiences can shift our moods and emotions. Reaching for a joyous memory can actually inspire you to move forward because it is proof that life can be wonderful.

Know that it is okay to take a stroll down memory lane today if it puts a smile on your face.

312

Tip of the Day

"Create your own sacred space today!"

Each of us needs a little piece of territory that we can call our own sanctified space that is special to us. It is a location that you can go to whenever you want. This space can be anywhere: in your home, the great outdoors or even a public location that you share with other people. A sacred space is where you go to unwind, just be, reflect and re-energize. It is a location you choose based on your terms.

Consider creating a sacred space just for you today.

313

Tip of the Day

"Take time today to find what you have in common with everyone you meet!"

Focusing on the commonalities you share with other people, instantly increases your overall level of compassion. This also reduces fears of interpersonal relationships and improves the quality of the daily interactions required to be and feel successful in all areas of your life. You also begin to realize the unity and connectedness between you and everyone else in the world.

Notice what you have in common with others today.

314

Tip of the Day

"Become a master inventor for your life today!"

A master inventor is someone who lives in infinite possibilities with no boundaries or restrictions to what he or she can create. A master inventor focuses on desired results despite being surrounded by people who create self-imposed limitations. You are a master inventor, yet you may not even know it!

Contemplate how you can master your status as an inventor today.

315

Tip of the Day

"Consider the possibility today that frustration is a step in the right direction!"

Frustration is good. Yes, you read that correctly. Frustration is awareness and awareness is a positive step toward change. It means you know what you do not want and that you want to shift direction to putting your focus and faith into results you desire.

Frustration today means you are a decision away from a brighter tomorrow.

316

Tip of the Day

"Take the helm today as the CEO and run the operations of the enterprise that is You, Incorporated!"

To take charge of your life observe as many aspects of yourself as you can. This process is called introspection and if applied with due diligence, awakens you to how you are running the business that is your life. Observe, without judgment, your thoughts, feelings and behavior patterns.

Take charge of your life today by paying attention to the mechanics of the business that is You, Incorporated.

317

Tip of the Day

"Know your true inner purpose today!"

Outer purposes, whatever we are inspired to create in the physical world, vary from one person to the next and can change over each of our lifetimes; however, as human beings we all have one inner purpose: *to enjoy what life offers us through what is the 'human experience.'* Misery is no one's purpose. Neither is suffering. Joy is everyone's true inner purpose. No more excuses!

Live your true inner purpose by being joyful today.

318

Tip of the Day

"Know the difference between confidence and arrogance today!"

A confident person possesses a firm belief in their abilities without the need to broadcast to the world, while an arrogant person will boast, has over-bearing pride and the need for self-importance. With confidence, you are trusting, certain and reliant upon yourself.

Develop confidence today by mastering the skills and expertise for you to believe in YOU.

319

Tip of the Day

"Let go of guilt in your life today!"

Guilt is a highly destructive emotion. It wears down and beats up people for as long as a lifetime. If guilt is playing a major role in your life, it is time to let it go. Stop living on a daily dosage of 'I should,' 'I have to,' 'I must' and 'If I had done it different.'

Free yourself emotionally and energize yourself by releasing guilt from your life today.

320

Tip of the Day

"Begin the process today of releasing your personal prejudices!"

Most of us have been conditioned to prejudge people we know or do not know because of how they appear to us, their beliefs, occupations, associations, and so on. Prejudices limit us. Remove prejudicial barriers by opening your mind and your heart.

Recognize and release today any prejudices you are holding on to and contribute to the emergence of a new world.

321

Tip of the Day

"Find a mentor today!"

No one accomplishes positive change and results alone. Whatever goals you have and whatever your vision is for your life, you will require a support team. You will also need sound advice from someone who is further along on the journey of success. If you seek great accomplishments and want to lead, it is imperative you communicate and collaborate with a mentor.

Be open to mentorship today.

322

Tip of the Day

"To have peace of mind today requires the choice for peace!"

The choice for peace is directly determined by how you perceive the world in any given moment. You can never have peace of mind when you spend most of your day in resistance by judging and criticizing. Consciously be open to curtailing and limiting your need to judge and criticize. Be okay with what is and take the appropriate action. You can only have peace of mind through acceptance and non-judgment.

Experience peace of mind today, and as a result, a more centered and positive you will emerge.

323

Tip of the Day

"Focus on completing the small steps today to achieve the big results you want for you!"

Sometimes, when we have big goals and dreams, and want big results, we overlook the importance of the small steps that can get us there. To achieve what we want requires a persistent and consistent effort. Small action steps, achieved over time, create a cumulative effect.

Take one small action step today to achieve the big results you want.

324

Tip of the Day

"Do not underestimate your power to create positive changes today!"

Most people see themselves as powerless when it comes to creating positive changes in their lives. They will come up with an endless stream of excuses about why they are the exception to the 'creating positive change rule.' *Excuses do not count!* The power to change is just a decision away.

Re-evaluate your power to change today.

325

Tip of the Day

"Give your life new meaning today!"

To provide your life with new meaning and purpose requires you to identify who is important to you and what you value most. Life lacks meaning when we minimize or ignore the value of whom and what is present in our lives. Acknowledge who is important and what you value most of all. Extend gratitude, appreciation and love to those 'valuables.' Identifying these values will invigorate your sense of purpose.

Give new meaning to the life that you are living today.

326

Tip of the Day

"Acknowledge the eternal aspect of who you are today that is forever young!"

Within each of us is an essence of what we are that is forever young. It is the piece of all of us that is ageless, changeless and eternal. Talk to any elderly person and they will tell you that there is a part of them that still feels like a child or teenager. They are referring to their ageless self. Be open to living your life from that 'forever young' perspective. When you live life this way you realize there are no timetables, deadlines or restrictions on what you can be and what you can do or have.

From today forward, live life from that part of you that is forever young.

327

Tip of the Day

"Become acquainted with who you truly are today!"

Each of us is a unique, individualized spirit; however, we are conditioned to strive, struggle and plod through life with the hope that at some point we will finally 'be somebody' by focusing on fame, fortune, accolades and acknowledgments. The only result of this approach is that it provides you with a false identity. Know that you already are somebody!

Highlight the positive aspects, traits and characteristics of who you are today and say hello to the real you.

328

Tip of the Day

"Open up today to using the healing powers you already possess!"

Every human being has the capacity to heal either physically or emotionally. There is no exception to this rule unless you believe you are powerless. To heal is the willingness to rise above any so-called obstacle in your life's path. There is no disease, disorder or distress that cannot be eradicated, erased or eliminated. You possess the power to heal.

Be open to activating your natural ability to heal today.

329

Tip of the Day

"Commit to being a peak performer today!"

Peak performance is producing results at the optimum level. This requires presence. By *'living in the now'* we create and perform at much higher levels of productivity. This is vastly different than attempting to perform while preoccupied with negative thoughts and stories about the past or the thoughts and worries based in future. Clear your mind. Be present.

Begin the process of becoming a peak performer today.

330

Tip of the Day

"In your attempt to create positive, successful results today, notice whether you are focused on cost or value!"

Most people fixate on the cost of 'things' or the opportunity to improve the quality of life. Successful people focus on value. Value is the payoff, the payout, the end result you want. Focus on cost and you never get the 'goodies.'

Shift your focus today, if necessary, from 'the cost of living' to the value of 'the life you want to live.'

331

Tip of the Day

"Know who is in control of YOU today!"

Do you know who is in control when it comes to your life? Is it you who is reading this right here and now or is it your mind with its thoughts and beliefs based in past and future? Your mind is in control when these thoughts control how you feel and act. If this is your situation, it may be time to change your mind about your mind. To do this, simply give yourself permission now to operate the control panel that is your mind. Awaken to the truth that you can change your thoughts and beliefs. You are only at the mercy of your mind if you allow it to be so.

Take back your life today by controlling the machine that is your mind.

332

Tip of the Day

"Remove the presence of certain conditions as requirements for being happy today!"

When we live our lives in a conditional state we are always seeking happiness outside ourselves. Conditions are blocks and barriers. They destroy opportunity for you to live in peace and authenticity. With conditions there can be no unconditional love, which is true love, in your life.

Be willing to start eliminating conditions for happiness in your life today.

333

Tip of the Day

"Consider the possibility today that you chose your parents prior to your birth!"

The idea of choosing your parents may stir you a bit; however, know that your family history is the most significant portion of your life curriculum. Our parents are our greatest teachers because they more than anyone else provide us with the spiritual lessons and healing we need in this lifetime. We all come in to this world with a particular purpose. Inherent in our purpose or mission are lessons for us to learn and transcend so we can accomplish our goals in this lifetime.

Take time today to consider why you may have chosen your parents in this lifetime.

334

Tip of the Day

"Ponder this statement today: If love hurts, then it is not love!"

Oddly, most modern cultures and societies associate love with pain. This is a misconception that confuses neediness with love. When love 'hurts' it is an indicator that you feel incomplete as long as that person or relationship is absent from your life. Pure love has no pangs of hurt associated with it.

Clearly define love for yourself and your life today.

335

Tip of the Day

"Yesterday's best laid plans can always be changed and enhanced today!"

Nothing, including plans, goals and purposes, is *'etched in stone.'* Change is one of life's constants. When your plans appear to go awry and are not producing the results you desire, know that you have the ability and capability to lay down a new and improved one.

If necessary, apply your innate talent and wisdom to create a new plan today.

336

Tip of the Day

"Respond positively rather than reacting negatively today to negative feedback and advice!"

Be willing to take a new approach to negativity from other people or from your own thoughts and feelings. Allow negativity to inspire you to rise to any occasion and be more determined than ever to succeed. Know that anything is possible and that naysayers are likely to always be negative.

Respond with positivity to negativity today.

337

Tip of the Day

"Allow your sacred goodness to radiate out today!"

Within all of us lies the truth of who we are. This truth is your unconditioned Self. The unconditioned Self is the part of you that is changeless no matter what appears to be happening in any moment of your life. Consciously tap in to the sacred YOU as often as possible and notice positive changes in your life.

Share the goodness that is you today.

338

Tip of the Day

"Be open to mixing and mingling with other people today!"

When we isolate ourselves, we do so to protect ourselves from being hurt, exposed or humiliated based on stories we have told ourselves and experiences we have had. Living a full life requires socializing with others. Develop a social skill that provides joy to both you and others: learn an instrument, a new game or sport and even conversation. Feel and move through the fear to be social.

Develop the skills to be proficient today for the mix and mingle process of socializing with others.

339

Tip of the Day

"Take time out today for a period of serenity!"

Everyone needs to refuel, recharge and rejuvenate during certain times of the day. Serenity is a state of calm and tranquility. How you achieve this state is unimportant; that you commit to being serene is essential. Take deep breaths, read, walk in nature, or meditate. These are just some of the many ways to create serenity.

Commit to a respite from the daily routine today by taking a serenity break.

340

Tip of the Day

"Know what you absolutely need today to live a full and joyous life every day!"

Beyond the obvious physical needs of shelter, food, water and clothing, there are also spiritual needs to be fulfilled. These essential spiritual needs are love, recognition, creativity, esteem, productivity and security. Without your spiritual needs being met, you cannot reach your full potential.

Reach your full potential and live a full life today by acknowledging and beginning to satisfy your own spiritual needs.

341

Tip of the Day

"Create a happiness disclaimer for your relationships today!"

To disclaim means to renounce responsibility. Simply knowing that you are not responsible for making others happy creates a mental happiness disclaimer. Sign this disclaimer in your mind or even put it on paper and begin to release yourself from feeling guilty and the role of being the producer of happiness for others.

Commit to following your happiness disclaimer today.

342

Tip of the Day

"Learn the truth today about seeking satisfaction!"

Satisfaction, like peace, is an 'inside job.' When you believe your only source of satisfaction is accomplishments, achievements and victories, you will likely live life in a state of dissatisfaction. We all want to create desired results; however, true satisfaction is gratitude for all that we have and 'what is' in any given moment.

Be satisfied with 'now' and feel satisfaction today.

343

Tip of the Day

"To experience true forgiveness today or any day simply requires willingness!"

Real forgiveness is easier than you may believe. All it takes is your openness to surrendering and cease condemning. This includes erasing the habit of nursing old wounds. Forgiveness does not mean we condone inappropriate behavior. It is a process to free ourselves emotionally so we feel inner peace.

Be open to forgive today.

344

Tip of the Day

"Use the 'four-pronged approach' today to manifest the results you desire!"

In any area of your life where you are not achieving your desired results, you may want to consider using the 'four-pronged approach'. This simple formula gives you a one hundred percent guarantee to create whatever it is you want. This technique has four essential factors that must be in total alignment with each other. They are: the thoughts you think, the emotions you feel, the words you speak and the action you take. When these factors are in alignment you will create anything you desire!

Apply this 'four-pronged approach' in your life today and manifest whatever it is you desire.

345

Tip of the Day

"Choose to be more charitable to you today!"

True charity includes giving to you. The easiest way to being more giving toward yourself is to stop condemning other people in your own mind. Now, you may ask, how is giving to me connected to how I judge people? Believe it or not, the flaws we see in others are projections of how we see ourselves. Seek the goodness and worthiness in others to develop a deeper, stronger and desirable self-image.

See the value in others today as a way of being more charitable.

346

Tip of the Day

"Conduct an internal 'search party' today to identify what appears to be missing from your life!"

Be open to a 'search and find' process that can assist you to see what may be missing emotionally in your life. Ask yourself, "What is missing internally?" Is it trust? Is it faith? Is it compassion? Maybe it is courage or inspiration. Whatever it is, it can be found.

Send in a search party today and rescue your positive emotional state.

347

Tip of the Day

"Treat today and every day as a holy day!"

The modern world has a long list of dates we set aside as holidays commemorating famous births or special events. Truth be said, every day is a holiday; more specific, a *holy* day. This day is sacred because it affords each of us the opportunity for new beginnings. Do not shrug off today as 'just another day.'

Make today and each day to follow a holy day for you.

348

Tip of the Day

"Let go of using 'extreme measures' today!"

Extreme measures are unattainable standards you may have in place for yourself and others such as 'being the best,' 'always being perfect,' and 'always getting it right.' Extreme measures will paralyze you, stress you out and push you to emotional exhaustion. Simply give your best and know you are already perfect.

Feel more at peace by letting go of extreme measures today.

349

Tip of the Day

"Use the power of contemplation in your life today!"

Contemplation is an extremely valuable tool when considering the direction you want your life to go toward. It allows you to look at all the possibilities available to you from within. To maximize contemplation, listen to your heart. You can then create decisions with greater certainty.

When indecision is present today use the power of contemplation to create solutions for your life.

350

Tip of the Day

"Adopt a philosophy of sharing with others today!"

Be open to sharing. Be it an idea, knowledge, talent, experiences, material items. Rather than living from the notion of giving for the sake of receiving in return, live from the perspective of sharing. Sharing implies unlimited prosperity and abundance. It is acknowledging that there is enough for all of us and each situation creates a win-win result.

Share all that you are and have today.

351

Tip of the Day

"Recognize the 'energy source' that fuels your production tank today!"

Can you identify the power behind why you do what you do? Is it the search for approval and happiness? Is it prestige, fame, fortune? Using these 'energy sources' may get results; however, you will feel personally and emotionally unfulfilled. The preferred option is to tap into utter enthusiasm and inspiration. Only when you are fueled by enthusiasm and inspiration can you feel fulfilled.

Know the source of the fuel that is filling your production tank today.

352

Tip of the Day

"As you go through your day today notice the presence of loving feelings!"

Love, of the unconditional variety only, is a true indicator of living life purposefully. The absence of loving feelings from your life means you may have temporarily lost your spiritual way. Do not despair! No one can permanently lose the capacity to feel unconditional love.

Be open to allowing the presence of unconditional love to flow through you today.

353

Tip of the Day

"Be willing to drop the labels 'right' and 'wrong' from your life today!"

Living your life from the perspective of right or wrong always keeps you indecisive, perfectionistic, guilt-ridden or all of the above. Instead, speak and act 'appropriately.' Living life appropriately is approaching all relationships and situations from the heart, and intending to create results that benefit everyone.

Live 'appropriately' today.

354

Tip of the Day

"Switch from 'time' to 'love' today as a guiding power to heal all wounds!"

Time is not a guarantee for healing. Are there people in your life, past and present that you say you forgive for inappropriate activity, yet you cannot forget? Love, on the other hand, directed toward your source of pain, is the only true remedy to heal an emotional wound.

Why wait a lifetime to heal when you have the chance to do it through love today?

355

Tip of the Day

"Anticipate goodness in your life today!"

We all have a level of and focus on expectations that directly affect our reality. Anticipation, which is simply the process of imagining an outcome before it physically occurs, helps to amplify the level and focus of our expectations. Raise your energy vibration to receive what you want by expecting goodness in your life.

Anticipate only 'the good stuff' today.

356

Tip of the Day

"Share your opinions today 'by invitation only'!"

Most of us give our opinions freely. Our opinions allow us to be heard, look good and appear to be 'right.' Begin to live by a higher standard of behavior by giving opinions only when asked. This is when you can truly be of service because someone sees real value in what you have to say.

Adopt a 'by invitation only' policy when giving opinions today.

357

Tip of the Day

"Starting today, focus on one task at a time!"

In this fast-paced, warp speed, maniacal world we live in, has it become more difficult for you to complete tasks in a timely manner? Know this: completed tasks are results you desire. To create a result, decide when you want to achieve it and break it down into edible pieces. Recall the joke and its accompanying punch line: 'How do you eat an elephant?' 'One bite at a time!'

Focus on one task, one bite at a time today.

358

Tip of the Day

"Become a 'success seeker' today!"

What does success look like for you? Get very clear when formulating your answer. Once you have it, imprint what it feels like in your heart and how it appears in your mind. This process is extremely effective to achieve results. These imprints are touchstones or easy reminders that lead you to where it is you want to be.

Take time today to gain the clarity necessary to be a 'success seeker.'

359

Tip of the Day

"Issue a 'no excuses' policy for your life today!"

How much time do you spend making excuses? Rather than expending your emotional well-being on excuses that begin with 'I am not...,' 'I do not...,' 'I cannot...,' 'I have not...,' commit to creating positive changes in your life by affirming what you want. Use phrases of certainty: 'I am..,' 'I do...,' 'I can...,' 'I have...'

Put a 'no excuses' policy into effect today.

360

Tip of the Day

"To experience success in your life today realize the value of preparation!"

To be prepared means that you have laid down the groundwork for the results you desire for your life. Without preparation, your results will be mediocre at best. Preparation is focus. Preparation breeds order, consistency and fuels persistence.

Include preparation in the equation today to create the success you want.

361

Tip of the Day

"Allow happiness to come from any direction today!"

When you believe that happiness can only occur from the direction you want, you miss all other opportunities for happiness. By placing conditions on happiness, you will always be seeking it. Making happiness a future event never allows you to be happy now.

Check the conditions of your life today and realize the many opportunities you have for happiness.

362

Tip of the Day

"Make a decision today for you by YOU!"

You may ask for opinions from others to make a decision because you do not trust yourself. Decision-making is a process you want to master if you seek to be self-assured, self-reliant and self-empowered. Why place your life in the hands of another when at the deepest level you know the choices appropriate for you?

Listen to your heart and make decisions for you by you today.

363

Tip of the Day

"Whatever you are selling today, know why people buy!"

It does not matter what you are selling: a product, service, an idea, advice, yourself. People buy for one reason only: the likeability of the salesperson. Success in sales is about strong relationships. Develop your relationships, believe in yourself and that you deserve to be compensated.

No matter what you are selling today, above all, see the value in YOU.

364

Tip of the Day

"Immunize yourself today from contracting emotional wounds!"

If you are easily hurt by the words and behavior of others, apply these suggestions for healing these 'wounds:' 1. Decide that the opinion of others is irrelevant to your happiness, 2. Accept that everyone will not like or approve of you, 3. Relax and let go of negativity absorbed from others.

Take a dose of self-esteem today and cure your emotional wounds.

365

Tip of the Day

"Remove the stress that is present in your life today!"

It appears that we become stressed because of *who said this* or *who did that*, or some event or result did not turn out as we planned. At a deeper level, we are stressed for one reason only: we have a strong need to be in control. When you give up control, you eliminate stress.

Relinquish control today and notice how stress fades from your life.

About the Authors

Jon Satin and Chris Pattay are co-founders of Possibility Coaches, LLC. Since 2002, they have assisted individuals and business owners worldwide to rise above limitations and create the results they want both personally and professionally.

Jon and Chris are entrepreneurs and have built several businesses over the last two decades. They have extensive experience in business and personal development. They have trained thousands of people in the fields of personal growth, entrepreneurship and success. They are Life, Relationship and Business Coaches. Their approach is simple and practical and can be used by anyone in any or all areas of his or her life.

Like most people, Jon and Chris have personally experienced the ups and downs of life. Using proven methods during years of training, they were able to transform themselves from the inside-out and currently teach others how to do the same.

They facilitate a variety of venues including seminars, workshops and classes focusing on creating healthy relationships, becoming a master communicator, and experiencing true success, balance and inner peace in life. They also maintain a private practice where they conduct one-on-one sessions with clients by phone, Skype or in-person.

To contact Jon and Chris visit their websites:
www.PossibilityCoaches.com & www.TheTeamForSuccess.com

Follow their blog at www.PossibilityCoaches.net

Join their Synergetic Success Online Program
at: www.SynergeticSuccess.com

Possibility Coaches™
The Life, Relationship and Business Experts

The Possibility Coaches, Jon Satin and Chris Pattay offer one-on-one personal Life, Relationship and Business Coaching.

Their unique approach to Coaching can assist anyone who is experiencing challenges in any area of their life and in ALL their relationships.

The Possibility Coaches provide an environment that creates SOLUTIONS for anyone seriously seeking positive change. Their coaching programs produce RESULTS!

Sessions are by phone, Skype or in-person.

To learn more:
www.PossibilityCoaches.com *and*
www.TheTeamForSuccess.com

Follow their blog at:
www.PossibilityCoaches.net

Join The Possibility Coaches,
Jon Satin and Chris Pattay, for their
Synergetic Success Online Program

www.SynergeticSuccess.com